AF352634

Local Party Organizations in the Twenty-First Century

Local Party Organizations in the Twenty-First Century

Douglas D. Roscoe and Shannon Jenkins

An earlier version of chapter 4 was published in *Publius* 44(3) (2014): 519–540.

Published by State University of New York Press, Albany

For information, contact State University of New York Press, Albany, NY
www.sunypress.edu

Production, Ryan Morris
Marketing, Michael Campochiaro

Library of Congress Cataloging-in-Publication Data

Roscoe, Douglas D., 1969–
    Local party organizations in the twenty-first century / Douglas D. Roscoe and Shannon Jenkins.
        pages cm
    Includes bibliographical references and index.
    ISBN 978-1-4384-5949-3 (hardcover : alk. paper)
    ISBN 978-1-4384-5951-6 (e-book)
    1. Political party organization—United States.   2. Local elections—United States. 3. Politics, Practical—United States.   4. United States—Politics and government—21st century.   I. Jenkins, Shannon, 1971–   II. Title.

JK2271.R67 2016
324.273'11—dc23   2015009215

10 9 8 7 6 5 4 3 2 1

Contents

Tables and Figures

Tables

Figures

Acknowledgments

As with any book, we owe a debt of gratitude to a great many people. First, the intellectual roots of this project stem back to our days as graduate students, when we worked on the Election Dynamics Project with John Frendreis and Alan Gitelson. We are grateful for their mentoring and also recognize that the many hours we spent stuffing envelopes and coding data for the Election Dynamics Project taught us how to work long and hard to see a project come to fruition.

Once we got the idea to follow the lead of John and Alan and do our own survey, our initial pilot study was supported by a small research grant from the American Political Science Association. While we do not use our pilot data in this book, the support we received from this grant was instrumental in helping us refine our survey and helped confirm the notion that we had a good project here.

Our work has also been supported by administrators and colleagues at the University of Massachusetts Dartmouth. In particular, we are grateful for grants to support our survey and travel to conferences to present preliminary findings, sabbaticals to facilitate the writing of this book, and institutional policies that facilitated hiring undergraduate students as research assistants. Lindsay Hughes Tallman, Julie Leimert, Samantha Egge, Megan Libby, Ryan Gallagher, Betsy Rivera, Ryan Carreiro, Stephanie Capone, Erin McQuaid, John Cotreau, Chris Maderios, and Mac Denaro all played a role in helping us collect, organize, and analyze data. This project would have taken even longer than it has without their work.

The feedback we received on this project at professional conferences and from our colleagues over the years led to definite improvements in our manuscript. In particular, Tom Carsey, Neil Christiansen, Peter Francia, Marjorie Hershey, Matt Ingram, Seth Masket, Dan Shea, and Dick Winters provided useful feedback at various stages of our project. Thanks also to Michael Rinella, Ryan Morris, and the rest of the team at State University of New York Press for guiding this project to print.

We are also grateful for the willingness of so many party officials to participate in and support our project. Many state party leaders shared email addresses with us when they were not available on the web. Hundreds of local party chairs responded to our surveys and spent time with us on the phone, elaborating on the information they provided to us in those surveys. Without their willingness to be "poked and prodded," there would be no book.

Finally, there is no doubt in our minds that we would not have been able to complete this book without the support of our families. We are eternally grateful to Ann and Rich Bokor, Bill and Judy Jenkins, and Don and Isabelle Roscoe for the many years they put up with us. Thanks for your love and support. And last but certainly not least, we dedicate this book to our children, Quinlan and Berkley, who have had to listen to Mom and Dad debate and argue about political parties for far longer than any children should have to endure. We love you guys.

CHAPTER I

Party Organizations in Their Environment

In 1972, longtime *Washington Post* journalist David Broder published a book he titled *The Party's Over: The Failure of Politics in America.* The cover is perfectly illustrated, the GOP elephant and the Democratic donkey looking a little green after what appears to be a night of overindulgence, booze bottles scattered across the floor. The text carries on the theme, arguing the parties have lost their vitality in an American political process that features candidate-centered campaigns vying for the votes of dealigned voters unmoored from traditional partisan identities and loyalties. The marginalization of parties was troubling to Broder because he saw the parties as the only vehicles for enacting major policy changes. With the parties hung over, government would be rendered incapable of collective action.

Hindsight always provides an illuminating perspective, and we can now see that the party was just getting started. "What this country needs is some unvarnished political partisanship," Broder wrote at the time in an *Atlantic Monthly* article echoing the themes of the book (Broder 1972b, 33). Wish granted. In 2015, partisan vitriol has seemed to reach a new zenith. Party voting in Congress has climbed to new highs, reflecting the polarization of the congressional party caucuses and the increasing cohesion within them (McCarty, Poole, and Rosenthal 2006). Mass party identification has rebounded somewhat, but, more importantly, it has come to be more realigned with ideological viewpoints (Levendusky 2009). Ticket splitting has declined substantially from its peak in the early 1970s when Broder was writing about disintegrating parties. A red-state-versus-blue-state mindset has seemingly set in over the country.

While most Americans who pay at least some attention to politics are aware of the increasingly partisan political environment, few probably know what has happened to the party *organizations* during this time frame. As Key

1

(1958) pointed out many years ago, the political parties in the United States are composed of three parts: party-in-the-electorate, party-in-government, and party organizations. Pundits and the public alike have tended to fixate on the first two, mainly because they are more visible. Partisanship in Congress is a common feature in the news, and public opinion polling keeps the public aware of its shifting party affiliations. But party organizations are less visible to the general public. Political scientists, however, have paid more attention to this component of the parties, and their findings run counter to broader perceptions of party degeneration. Despite the proclamations of the parties' demise, these organizations continued a trajectory of increasing institutionalization and activity through the 1980s and 1990s.

Fueled by an energized fundraising capacity, the national party committees arrived in the 21st century as mature and highly effective organizations. The national parties had become "fiscally solvent, organizationally stable, and larger and more diversified in their staffing" (Herrnson 2002, 54). Their new organizational capacity meant a greater role in candidate recruitment, campaign training and management, public opinion research, campaign advertising, fundraising, and grassroots activity (Sabato and Larson 2002). Their new status also allowed them a bigger role in helping state and local party organizations to build their capacity. State party organizations matured considerably during this period as well. By the end of the century, almost all state parties had permanent headquarters, professional and specialized staffing, and ample budgets (Bibby 2002). These structural improvements allowed a great expansion of activity in areas like fundraising, training, advertising, recruitment, and grassroots mobilization (Aldrich 2000).

This institutionalization was also evident among local party organizations, which are the subject of this book. In fact, local party organizations were substantially more mature and active in the late 1970s than they were in the 1960s, and this trend of increasing local party strength continued into the 1980s (Cotter et al. 1984; Gibson et al. 1985; Gibson, Frendreis, and Vertz 1989). Research in the 1990s verified that local party organizations were still strong and active in the electoral arena. Frendreis and Gitelson (1999) found that, compared to the 1980s, local party organizations were as structurally developed and were more active programmatically in the 1990s.

Rather than being sidelined by the changes to campaigns that Broder documented, party organizations in the 1980s and 1990s found new ways to be useful to key actors in the political process. But in the years since the 1990s, much has changed in the political environment. The laws regulating campaign finance have been transformed in major ways, shifting the currents of campaign dollars. The internet has become a powerful tool for political action. And, amid the din of media and electronic communication, grassroots campaigning has reemerged as a key strategy. Given these changes, a fresh examination of political party organizations is in order. This book focuses on these organizations in America's local communities—in the counties, towns, and districts across the country. Since the rise of mass party organizations in the mid-19th century, local organizations have been the heart and soul of American parties. They are the place where common people have always engaged in party activity. They are also the place where candidates have often gone for help getting elected. But are local parties still as vibrant and central to the political process today as they have been historically? Is there still a place for local party organizations in the electoral environment of the 21st century?

A Changing Political Landscape

The survival of party organizations, even amid seemingly existential threats, is a theme recurring throughout American history. Almost a century earlier, Progressive reformers took aim at party organizations that had metastasized into party machines. Fed up with the inefficiencies and corruption perpetuated by machine politics, reformers gutted many of the tools party organizations relied on to exert influence on the electoral process. The introduction of the government-printed, secret ballot and the replacement of patronage with merit hiring systems removed the party's ability to arrange quid pro quo transactions with voters. Nonpartisan local elections removed the party's ballot gatekeeping role in many cities, and the introduction of the direct primary seemingly eliminated the organization's role in nominations, transferring this power to the party-in-the-electorate. Writing in the wake of the Progressive reforms, Frances Kellor predicted the atrophy of the party—at least its traditional role dealing with campaigns and elections:

> The direct primary, the abolition of conventions, fusion in municipal affairs, the commission form of government and similar movements are making the party less powerful. If the party is to survive as an instrument of power and as a means of expressing the will of the people there must be an expansion elsewhere. (Kellor 1914, 883)[1]

Despite these Progressive Era threats to party organizations, state and local party organizations persisted, albeit in different forms. The grip of the party machines on electoral politics weakened, but party organizations did not suddenly vanish. However, continued changes in the political environment forced parties to adapt yet again. The rise of mass media in the 1950s and 1960s led to the emergence of candidate-centered campaigns and continued worries about the fate of political parties, as articulated by Broder. The introduction of the McGovern-Fraser reforms in the Democratic Party, which constrained the ability of state and local party leaders to select delegates for the national party convention, were also seen as fundamental threats to party organizations. Yet parties still thrived, adapting to these changes in the political environment to continue their essential role in electoral politics in the 1980s and 1990s. Despite continued threats to the vitality of party organizations and despite continued concerns about the demise of political parties, party atrophy never occurred, even at the local level, where party organizations are least institutionally mature.

But the environment never remains static for long, and so we must continue to reconsider parties and their role in the American political process. We believe three key recent changes in the electoral environment may have had a profound impact on local parties and make this reconsideration necessary.

First, as Frendreis and Gitelson (1999) note, local party organizations in the past have focused on fostering connections between candidates and resources, with money being one such critical resource. The passage of the Bipartisan Campaign Reform Act (BCRA) in 2002, however, eliminated the flow of soft money from national to state and local party organizations (Bibby and Holbrook 1996; La Raja 2003). There was disagreement over what impact the BCRA would have on state and local parties, but there was consensus that the law's passage would alter the functioning of party organizations and the relationships among them (La Raja, Orr, and Smith 2006). The elimination of soft money meant parties had to work harder to raise more hard money to maintain previous levels of fundraising, so this environment created more incentives for entrepreneurial thinking (Dwyre et al. 2007). Ultimately, as La Raja, Orr, and Smith (2006) show, the effect of BCRA on state parties was to increase voter mobilization efforts and to decrease issue ad activity. Little is known, however, about the nature of fundraising and financial activity among local parties in the aftermath of BCRA and subsequent changes in campaign finance brought about by Supreme Court decisions.

In addition, the rise of the internet has changed the electoral environment. Candidates increasingly use the internet to connect with voters as well as to raise money, and voters are increasingly turning to the internet as a source of campaign information (Farnsworth and Owen 2004; Williams et al. 2005). Many local party organizations have begun to maintain their own website, separate from the state party organization, and have begun to use social networking tools like Facebook and Twitter. However, little is known about how widespread these tools are among local parties. The development of these cheap and effective means of directly communicating with voters and party loyalists may have provided local parties with new ways to reach out and attract activists and supporters.

Finally, recent election cycles have seen the reemergence of sophisticated canvassing and voter mobilization operations (Bergan et al. 2005). Hogan (2002) notes that during the 1990s many of the local parties' traditional grassroots functions gave way to service-oriented candidate assistance. During this period, party efforts were directed more toward candidates than voters (Frendreis and Gitelson 1999). However, in the last several elections, there has been a renewed emphasis on grassroots activity in electoral campaigns, with notable increases in door-to-door canvassing and voter mobilization, particularly among the presidential candidates. Bush political operatives, under the direction of Karl Rove, developed the 72-Hour Strategy in the 2002 midterm election as a way of piloting a major grassroots operation that would be used again in 2004. Democrats, while traditionally more committed to mobilization activity, also developed particularly extensive operations in 2004. And, of course, these trends continued in 2008 and 2012, particularly on the Democratic side, where the Obama campaign developed a remarkable grassroots operation. These changes may reflect a growing sense that, as the country polarizes, the portion of the electorate amenable to persuasion may be shrinking and so campaigns must focus on mobilizing their bases (Bergan et al. 2005). In the end, the renewed focus on voter mobilization efforts in recent elections may mean the resources local party organizations have the most access to, namely, motivated volunteers, are increasingly important. Combined with the loss of soft money, this new strategic imperative may mean state parties and candidates—state, local, and national—are focusing more on working with these local organizations to utilize their large pools of volunteers.

Organizational Evolution

Before considering how these recent environmental changes have affected local parties, it is worth reflecting on the nature of local party organizations and the general process by which they adapt. Why have parties persisted so well in the United States in the face of all these seemingly fatal threats? To answer this question, it is useful to begin with a theoretical exploration of organizational change at a general level. The adaptation of all organizations to their environment occurs in ways that parallel the adaptation of biological populations, and this realization has spawned an extensive literature on organizational evolution and ecology. This theoretical perspective is helpful in illuminating how parties have been successful at adaptation.

Organizational evolution is a process of relatively durable change in a population of organizations. The most important process in evolution is the adaptation of forms (Aldrich 1979; Stanley 1979). Forms are organizational structures or functional repertoires that describe a set of organizations in a population. Nelson and Winter (1982) refer to these regular and predictable patterns of behavior as "routines" that serve as the genes of an organization. Over time, adaptation occurs as less successful forms die out and successful forms persist.

The key to understanding organizational evolution is describing the adaptation process. For adaptation to occur, there must be three processes: variation, selection, and retention (Aldrich 1979; Campbell 1965). Populations of organizations must contain some diversity (variation), and some of these forms must function better in the environment (selection). Finally, these more functional forms must then persist over time (retention).

It is important to point out that theorists of organizational evolution perceive an actual process of natural selection at work. As Lewis and Steinmo (2012, 315) put it, "We do not use evolution as a metaphor." Organizational evolution can be viewed as an example of universal Darwinism, generalized Darwinism, or universal selection theory (Bickhard and Campbell 2003; Campbell 1965; Cziko 1995; Dawkins 1983; Hodgson 2005; Nelson 2007). Wherever there is variation, selection, and retention within populations of individual entities, there is a true process of evolution. Biological evolution is but one manifestation of this broader class of change, with specific biological mechanisms driving variation, selection, and retention.[2]

Of course, evolution does not unfold identically in different contexts (Lewis and Steinmo 2012). One key difference is the source of variation in a population. In biological populations, the key adaptation process is Darwinian natural selection.[3] In this process, variation arises from random mutations in the genetic code; most mutations reduce an organism's chances for survival and procreation, but some increase the chances, and these forms are selected and retained by the offspring. There is an ongoing, selective attrition at the individual level, a survival of the fittest. In Darwinian processes, individual organisms do not change over their lifetime in ways that are retained by future generations.

Some theorists emphasize this kind of Darwinian process among organizations. This perspective focuses on the extent to which organizations are burdened with substantial inertia, which limits meaningful change at the level of the individual organization (Carroll 1984; Hannan and Freeman 1989). Organizations arise, are imprinted with a form early on, and then succeed (persist) or fail (die) based on how well suited their forms are for their environment. Carroll (1984, 73) calls this perspective the "selection approach to evolution" and notes an emphasis on population-level phenomena. The work on organizational ecology, which seeks to understand organizational populations within certain niches, falls into this category. A good example of this approach is the work on interest group populations by Lowery and Gray (1995; 2000), which seeks to understand the size and diversity of interest group populations within the states.

In this view, individual organizations do not alter form substantially during their existence. The adaptation of *forms* arises because at any given point the organizations that have persisted have a successful (adaptive) form and the ones that died out had less successful forms. Selection happens because of the natural diversity occurring as organizations in a population are *created* and the differential effect that the environment has on organizations with different forms. This process works well for explaining adaptation among some types of organizations, such as business firms. For example, the restaurant industry is marked by great diversity, achieved by entrepreneurs realizing various concepts for restaurants. Each restaurant tends to maintain a singular identity over its life, but mortality is high, so unsuccessful forms die out and successful ones persist.[4] The successful form is retained within the existing restaurant but may also be copied by new restaurants—for instance, the fundamentals of the fast-food franchise form created by McDonald's (e.g., counter service with quick delivery of food) have remained virtually unchanged and have been copied by many other restaurants.

Alternatively, the adaptation of forms need not arise only through mortality and birth processes. It is possible that existing organizations change their form during their lifetime and that these changes are retained. After all, organizations are created and maintained by people, and people have the cognitive capacity to shape organizations in ways they reasonably expect will be adaptive. "Humans' creative capacities and problem-solving abilities are important mechanisms for generating continued variation in human social systems" (Lewis and Steinmo 2012, 316). We strive to improve our organizations. "Much learning, adaptation, and change take place within organizations" (Meyer 1990, 301). People are able to reflect on the routines of their organizations and alter them in ways they expect will improve performance; this creates the "mutations" that lead to variation in the organizational population (Nelson and Winter 1982). Efforts to manage the culture of organizations can be seen as an example of attempts to encourage organizational adaptation. Research has demonstrated that organizational culture is linked to organizational effectiveness (Denison 1990); organizational leaders who are aware of this often seek to manage their organizational culture in order to increase organizational effectiveness through mechanisms such as employee hiring processes, rituals, and formal codes of behavior (Gibson et al. 2002; Luthans 1995).

Of course, managing organizational culture is difficult (Gibson et al. 2002), which illustrates the limits on the ability of humans to manage organizational adaptation. Though we may attempt intentional change, we lack "the capacity to fully predict the consequences of any particular institutional change" (Lewis and Steinmo 2012, 322). Some of these mutations are adaptive, and others are not. Furthermore, whether these mutations are adaptive may depend on the environment in which these adaptations occur. For example, in the context of organizational culture, Denison (1990) notes that some organizational cultures that are adaptive in one environment may not be particularly effective in a different environment. Hence, this variation in both adaptations and environments sets the stage for selection.

This kind of change might be viewed as Lamarckian selection, in that organizations that have maladaptive forms can *learn* new approaches and develop into a new form that then persists within the continuing organizations and that may even be imitated by other organizations in the population (Hannan and Freeman 1989; Lewis and Steinmo 2012). Successful organizations are those that adopt, through innovation or imitation, more adaptive forms.

It is likely that in most organizational populations there are both Darwinian and Lamarckian processes at work, with the relative importance of each depending on the nature of the organization. However, for some kinds of organizations, Darwinian selection is essentially impossible. When the existence of organizations in a population is supported by external forces, there can be no selective mortality. As Perrow (1979, 242) put it, "we simply do not let schools and garbage collectors go out of business." Of course, Perrow's choice of examples underscores the extent to which organizations are never fully protected from death; garbage collection in many communities has been privatized since he wrote in 1979, and school restructuring options under No Child Left Behind allow state governments to replace public schools with charter schools, replace all of the school staff, or even contract with a private management company. For this reason, it is better to think about some organizations as being protected from mortality, to varying degrees, rather than being immortal.

Political party organizations enjoy this kind of protection. One major reason is that party organizations have a special legal status that protects them from mortality in a way not enjoyed by interest groups, business firms, or biological organisms. Parties are, at one level, strictly private organizations composed of private citizens coming together to engage in collective action. But their tight relationship with official governmental functions, particularly elections, has made them semi-public in practice—what Epstein (1986) terms "public utilities." Particularly since the Progressive Era, state laws have attempted to regulate party organizations in various ways. As Epstein (1986) notes, the adoption of the Australian ballot meant the government was responsible for printing the names of parties and their candidates on the ballots. This responsibility brings with it a need to determine what is and is not a political party and which candidates should have the right to attach their names to the parties on the official ballot.

Consequently, states had to issue regulations about ballot access that, at a minimum, identify which organizations are the "official" Democratic and Republican parties with the ability to nominate candidates. Of course, the direct primary largely has taken away this power from the party organizations and placed it in the hands of party voters, but in many ways this has tightened the link between the law and parties, as the state has entered the business of running (and paying for) the elections that nominate party candidates.

State regulations today may encompass very specific elements of party structure, such as "procedures for selecting officers, composition of party committees, dates and locations of meetings, and powers of party units" (Holbrook and La Raja 2013, 66). As just one example, Wyoming statute specifies the existence of county committees and precincts and the number of committeemen and committeewomen for each precinct; calls for regular county committee meetings and sets rules for the timing and notice for these meetings; establishes the selection process for the county committee chair and the delegates to the county and state conventions; delineates the composition and selection of state party committees; and mandates state party conventions, sets rules for these conventions, and even enumerates the specific powers of the convention, for instance, to nominate electors for presidential elections and to adopt a platform (Wyo. Stat. §22.4-1). Additionally, in the modern era of campaign finance regulation, state as well as federal laws have become involved in establishing the legal identity of political parties for the purposes of collecting and distributing election funds (sometimes from public funding programs).

These state laws, overall, greatly favor the two major parties over third parties. For example, they typically grant ballot access more-or-less automatically to the major parties, while requiring sometimes extremely burdensome petition requirements for third party candidates.[5] Federal campaign finance laws automatically qualify Democratic and Republican presidential nominees (and their parties' nominating conventions) for the public general election grant; minor parties must qualify by showing adequate vote share. Similar standards apply for state public funding programs.

The effect of this preference for major parties is that the law regulates party organizations differently than other types of organizations. Corporations and interest groups, for example, are subject to numerous laws and regulations at both the federal and state levels. But these laws apply to *classes* of organizations, not specific organizations. In contrast, because the law buttresses the two major parties, it effectively regulates particular Republican and Democratic organizations. As Epstein (1986) points out, this puts parties in the same protected class as heavily regulated public utilities. The presence of state and local parties "has been practically mandated by state law and their continued existence virtually assured" (Holbrook and La Raja 2013, 69).[6]

The place of local party committees is supported not only by these legal provisions but also by the internal rules of the parties overall. Local committees, state committees, and national committees are bound together by formal rules that define how the committees interrelate. National committee rules, for instance, specify how state parties may select their representatives to the national committees as well as how delegates are selected to national conventions. Similarly, state party rules delineate how local committees may select their officers, their representatives on the state committee, and their delegates to state conventions. Because of these rules, local committees can be said to exist as part of the larger web of party committees, even when there is little or no actual activity in these committees.

And, indeed, it is important to point out that the life support provided by state laws need not guarantee a meaningful existence for local party committees. They may become empty shells, doing very little, catatonic patients kept alive by machines. But they still exist as formal organizations, recognized by state party bylaws, state law, or both. This kind of dormancy describes, for instance, many local Republican organizations in the South throughout much of the 20th century. A Democratic county party chair in Maine whom we interviewed described a local party committee that had been very successful mobilizing a large group of local activists until its chair passed away. Subsequently, those activists were staying home during election season and the party became dormant. But the activist network was still there, and the county party still existed; a new leader could very easily revive that organization. These organizations never really died, in a formal sense. Instead, they persisted much like shell corporations—serving as a vehicle for party business but not really having any actual activity.

Because of these protections from mortality, any change among party organizations must result from Lamarckian change. Lamarckian change requires a mechanism of learning, a way in which organizations can gauge the possibilities for new forms, assess which will work better, and adopt wholly new structures and functional repertoires. Humans, of course, have the capacity to engage in these kinds of learning (Lewis and Steinmo 2012). As Schlesinger (1984, 390) puts it, parties "are perhaps best described as forms of organized trial and error." To understand party change, we must examine the individuals who drive this trial and error.

Party Organizers and the Party Exchange

Within party organizations, there are individuals who might be termed *party organizers*, who manage the organizational life of the party committees and push their organizations to try new ways of accomplishing their goals or even to attempt new goals. These individuals create the diversity of forms within the population of party organizations. Because of their key role in the adaption process, it is worth considering what motivates them.

We see the role of party organizers as similar to the role of interest group organizers in Salisbury's (1969) exchange theory of interest groups. In Salisbury's theory, group organizers package a set of selective benefits and seek members who will provide material support to the group in exchange for these benefits. The organizers take a sort of profit from this, either in money, as salary, or in terms of their own purposive satisfaction.

The role of the party organizer is slightly different, because the nature of parties is different. Though parties can be viewed like businesses selling a product to consumers, party organizations act more like wholesalers or distributors. Their activities often involve connecting the needs of different actors in the political sphere. Party organizers use the party organizations as a way of connecting pools of resources to unfilled or poorly filled political functions. Often, party organizations "market" not to voters but to other political elites who have specific needs in order to achieve their own goals (usually related to voters).

For example, party organizations often organize fundraising events at which candidates can solicit direct contributions from individuals or PAC leaders. One Democratic chair in a South Carolina party organization suggested this type of event was one of the most important activities in which it engages, because the party is able to leverage its credibility and network for the candidates. Similarly, local parties may be the source of various kinds of expertise, particularly for neophyte candidates. This might include legal advice, accounting assistance, or even polling. If the party cannot provide this help directly, it is likely to know which private consultants or firms would be best able to help a candidate. Even local party activists must be viewed as a brokered resource. Among the chairs we interviewed, many explained that the presidential campaigns would liaison with the local party committees, often in ways mediated by the state party leadership, to direct and coordinate local grassroots activity. As we will show in chapter 3, local parties are far less likely to engage voters directly through mass media than to provide supporting services to candidates or leverage their volunteers for grassroots campaign activity. Local parties do not run campaigns; they supply campaigns.

In this regard, we disagree with Schlesinger (1984), who adopts Downs's (1957, 25) definition of parties as a "team seeking to control the governing apparatus by gaining office in a duly constituted election." For Schlesinger, this team includes candidates, office holders, and, presumably, party organization leaders; it excludes voters. While this definition may be workable for the concept of *party*, it does not adequately capture what we mean by *party organization*.[7] The organizational apparatus is distinct from candidates and office holders. Chairs and officers in local, state and national party committees are very often not office holders or candidates themselves. Even when they are, they play distinct roles. Lumping the organizational and office-seeking parts of the party into a single team obscures what is really happening in the electoral process, especially in contemporary elections.

In the age of candidate-centered elections, candidates are more like private labels. Rarely do candidates even include their party affiliation on campaign material, websites, or ads. Candidates are independent operators. They are selling themselves to voters, each a small business (or large, in the case of presidential candidates). Party organizations do not sell candidates any more than Foxconn, the Chinese manufacturing firm, sells iPads. The role of the party organization is to support the candidates, in ways the candidates find useful.

As Frendreis and Gitelson (1993; 1999) explain, party organizations are *adaptive brokers* that make connections among elite actors who either have or seek electoral resources. Parties "often serve as brokers, facilitating the connection between candidate organizations and pools of necessary resources, such as money, expertise, and volunteers"; adaptation occurs as "party organizations respond to changes in their environment . . . by developing new capacities and altering the electoral roles they perform" (Frendreis and Gitelson 1999, 152). The individuals we are describing as party organizers are the people responsible for creating these new capacities and developing the new roles. They look for new functions and new sets of resources and find novel ways to connect them.

The emerging use of micro-targeting data is a good example. Both parties have developed very sophisticated databases—the RNC's Voter Vault and the DNC's DataMart/Demzilla databases—that contain detailed information about voters. At some point in the 1990s and early 2000s, forward-thinking individuals within the party organizations grasped the utility of this kind of database for targeting election appeals to voters. These data have been used by thousands of candidates. Similar kinds of innovation occur on a more mundane level in local parties on a regular basis. An organizer might decide to try decentralized cell-phone banking, or to canvass in a new location, or leaflet in the parking lot of the local youth soccer fields. Moreover, the internet has created new opportunities for party organizers to innovate. As we will see in chapter 3, many local parties have begun to assist candidates with online fundraising.

As with group organizers, party organizers take some form of profit. This profit can be purely purposive, accruing simply from the act of helping to fulfill functions that are congruent with the entrepreneur's purposive beliefs (Clark and Wilson 1961). The profit can also be material, as when employment opportunities are enhanced by one's position in the party. Monetary profit may be unethical, such as in party machines whereby money is funneled out of the resource-function connection and into the pocket of the party organizer. Profit can also be political, meaning the party leader increases his or her own ability to run for an elected office or gain employment in the political establishment at a later point. This kind of political profit is partly purposive, partly material, and partly serving ambition. But, in most cases, this is more like an investment than a dividend. Indeed, it's possible to think of these politically ambitious individuals as *party investors*. They provide their labor now in the hopes of accruing some future political benefit. A Democratic chair in Florida we interviewed described a set of "new, really young, savvy individuals who are very ambitious" and who compete to take charge of various party operations in order to make a name for themselves in the party establishment. These "field marshals" operate as managers and innovators within the party in order to "make their own path in the process," and they end up "jockeying for the state party positions, for the appointments, for the political consultant jobs in DC."

It is important to make a distinction between party organizers and party activists. The latter also engage in party activity in exchange for purposive, material, or solidary benefits, but from an organizational perspective, they must be viewed more as resources than as actors who direct those resources. Organizers are the leaders within the organization, frequently those with the most commitment to sustained organizational work, who typically occupy formal positions. They may have some political ambition for higher party offices or elective office themselves, and they are most likely tied into the elite networks within their communities, especially those connected to political and economic affairs. Party activists, in contrast, tend to be episodic participants in party affairs, being drawn into party activity around election time and sprung into action by the issues and personalities of the elections at hand. Activists may show up to make phone calls, hold signs at visibility events, deliver lawns signs, or go door-to-door talking with voters. But most will not attend local party committee meetings, and only a very few would consider holding an office within the party organization. As one Florida chair explained, there may be "fifty people who are more than willing to pick up a sign and knock on a door and pick up the phone and make a phone call, but usually only five of those people are willing to actually call the other volunteers and pull them together and motivate them and move them around." In contrast to the organizers, who ascend to permanent leadership positions within the organizations, the activists are electoral transients. As the Florida chair explained, "After the election, you lose so many people, because they're no longer fighting for anything." Of course, there are some activists who more regularly participate in party activity, and most party organizers likely were at some point activists who then decided to commit more fully to the party. There is perhaps more of a continuum than a clean set of categories, but the distinction between the two types is nonetheless still clear.

The distinction between organizers and activists bears some resemblance to that between professionals and amateurs (Conway and Feigert 1968), but only in part. Party activists, like those traditionally defined as amateurs, tend to be motivated by purposive and solidary benefits. And those individuals identified as professionals, with strong material motivations and ambitions for careers in politics, would certainly fall into the category we are describing here as party organizers. But not all organizers are professionals—many local party chairs are filled by committed ideologues who devote extensive amounts of their time for purely purposive gains, with no interest in climbing any ladder of political ambition.

Innovation and Adaptation

While activists provide their labor, organizers provide their leadership, and part of leadership is guiding an organization through periods of change and adaptation. How does this change and adaptation occur?

Some innovation occurs when longstanding leaders within the organization attempt new ways of doing things. For example, while the fundamentals of McDonald's business model have not changed, a customer from the 1950s would hardly recognize the McDonald's menu these days: smoothies, wraps, Happy Meals, and more all represent changes made by the corporation to remain relevant in today's changing fast-food landscape. Market research and attention to changing consumer tastes drove these changes. Denison (1990, 10) notes organizations that are externally focused and driven are better able to translate signals from the external environment into behavioral changes, increasing the organization's chances for survival and growth. So organizations, particularly those that are externally focused, may drive adaptation in recognition of the need to do things differently in order to thrive.

Among party organizations, this change may be top down, as when a national or state party works to produce changes in local party organizations, or it may be bottom up, as local parties try out different ways of engaging in party business. The Democrats' 50-state strategy is an example of change driven by the national parties. The party describes this strategy as "an ambitious effort to build the Democratic Party from the ground up in every single precinct, city and state in the country" (DNC 2014). Party leaders, recognizing the importance of strong party organizations on the ground, worked to build and change state and local party organizations. And news accounts largely praise this strategy for helping greatly with Obama's 2008 election efforts. Republicans, learning from the success of the Democrats, launched their own 50-state strategy after the 2012 elections (Hamby 2013), illustrating how organizations may seek to adapt based on feedback from the environment and by examining the actions of other successful organizations. State parties can also drive top-down innovation. A Republican chair in Georgia we interviewed reported an effort by the state party committee to target dormant county committees by identifying and supporting local politicos who might revive the local organizations.

Of course, while Hamby (2013) describes the efforts of the Republican National Committee to build local Republican organizations as a "bottom-up" effort, true bottom-up change may be initiated by local party officials seeking to do things differently. Like an old dog learning new tricks, local organizers may undertake entirely new and innovative activities or adopt changes from other party organizations. One Republican chair in Illinois revamped the local party bylaws in order to empower the midlevel leadership at the township level, providing a more effective connection between the county leaders and the precinct captains. As he explained, "Boss Hog–style politics isn't going to work here." State party conventions, which bring local party organizers and activists together, may be fertile grounds for information about successful adaptation, and, of course, local party organizers may learn from looking across the party aisle.

Alternatively, party innovation can occur when outsiders come into the organization and attempt to remake it. These outsiders might be viewed as party entrepreneurs and fall into a special class of party organizer. Entrepreneurs play a critical role, of course, in the natural selection process of other organizational populations—indeed, the term is usually applied to individuals launching business organizations. It is the risk-taking of entrepreneurs that creates the natural diversity of a population that allows selection processes to unfold. But, in most populations, entrepreneurs create a new organization with a distinctive form, and that organization will die or persist based on how adaptive that form is to the environment. In the case of parties, the entrepreneurs do not create new organizations but rather come into existing party organizations and push new forms onto them.

What drives these innovations in party organizations? Appleton and Ward (1997) identify a number of ways party organizations might be prompted to innovate. Occasions for innovation can be both periodic and accidental—for example, elections often prompt reflection, and major policy shifts can be a powerful stimulus for change. Usually, there is some disruption that creates disequilibrium, and this serves as the impetus for change. How well these stimuli are converted into innovation depends on a number of intervening factors, according to Appleton and Ward, among them internal factionalism, institutionalization, and fragmentation.

As noted earlier, party innovation, regardless of the nature and source, occurs within continually existing organizations. These circumstances might, at first glance, appear likely to dampen party adaptation. Many theorists of organizational change have emphasized that human organizations have tendencies to fall into regular patterns and become resistant to change (Carroll 1984; Hannan and Freeman 1989). However, there are three key features of political parties and the environment in which they reside that make them highly adaptable through Lamarckian processes.

First, the legal protections for parties mean fundamental organizational tasks are unnecessary. The practical consequence of maintaining life support for the party organizations is that there are very small startup costs for a party entrepreneur or little disincentive for leaders within a nonthriving organization to attempt change. The organization already exists. It has a formal structure, with formal connections to other organizations. It is well known and connected to a longstanding brand. Therefore, party innovators may find it easier to attempt a new form of organization than an interest group or business entrepreneur.

Second, these same legal regulations have increasingly meant local party committees are permeable organizations. Individuals can essentially self-select into membership. To become involved in a party organization, a person need do nothing more than show up at meetings (and perhaps register to vote in party primaries). Though historically parties were not always so unbounded, it has always been possible for individuals willing to do party work to get involved in local committees. In contrast, business firms select only employees they choose. Even interest groups are fairly bounded. Becoming truly involved in the organizational life of an interest group, beyond simply donating money, requires a much greater commitment and connection than showing up at the local party committee meeting. As a result, new ideas are easily injected into parties through new membership.

This permeability has meant that party entrepreneurs inject a dynamism into party organizations that may be lacking in other organizations. Organizations may tend toward ossification, as Hannan and Freeman (1989) assert. People resist change. But, the openness of party organizations helps overcome this.

Consider the example of a young, conservative activist who would like to help other conservatives get elected. To found an interest group, he would have to figure out the legal requirements for establishing a nonprofit corporation and would then have to recruit some other individuals to help with a membership drive. Like most membership drives, this would require a direct mail and/or email solicitation and so would necessitate a substantial up-front investment in cash. However, it would seem relatively easy for him to take a dormant local party organization and push it in new directions.

He might attend some meetings of the county Republican Party, network, get elected chair, and perhaps harness other local conservative activists for a new canvassing operation in aid of local Republican candidates. The organization is already there. Membership is already there, even if minimal. He could focus his entrepreneurial energies on developing the new organizational forms rather than on basic startup operations.

This example may be common, as the evidence suggests high levels of turnover among party organizers. Data from a 1996 survey of 673 local party chairs (the study is described in Frendreis and Gitelson 1999) reveal quite a lot of turnover. The median year at which the respondents first became chair was 1993, and 65% had started as chair in 1991 or later.

In addition to permanence and permeability, a third feature that promotes adaptation is the periodicity of regular elections. For business organizations, feedback may be nearly constant, supplied by sales and earnings figures; this constant data stream may reveal only incremental change and may make it difficult for businesses to engage in anything more than incremental adaptation. But for parties, feedback via elections occurs at periodic intervals and is typically quite dramatic and visible. Every two years (perhaps more frequently depending on the nature of state and local elections), parties must assess the results of their efforts and determine what adaptations are necessary in the wake of these results. Election results, particularly poor election results, provide the impetus for party strategic planning on a biennial basis. Dramatic losses can catalyze major organizational change.

And of course, the media feeds this critical self-reflection. A Google search in 2014 for "end of the Republican Party" suggests autofills of "2008" and "2012." Pundits liked to speculate about the coming death of the Republican Party in the wake of both Obama elections. But as noted earlier, the Republicans have adapted and remain, much to the chagrin of the Obama administration, a potent force in US politics. Like Mark Twain's, the death of the Republican Party has been greatly exaggerated, as illustrated by the 63 seat pick-up in the House in the 2010 midterm elections and the return of the Senate to Republican control in 2014. Furthermore, elections may induce entrepreneurs into party adaptation. Frustration over lackluster party efforts may finally motivate entrepreneurs into activity.

Consequently, large or unexpected electoral losses naturally induce party reflection about what went wrong. Democrats engaged in such soul-searching after dramatic Republican gains in 1994, as they wondered how to develop their own Contract with America. And Republicans have engaged in their own soul-searching about the role of the Tea Party after the 2012 elections. Parties seek to determine what they could (or can) do differently.

Regular national elections, and the swings that often accompany them, mean that no party organizations are immune to this self-reflection. Even though gains and losses may be concentrated in specific areas or regions, the national nature of these results often induces across-the-board reflection, meaning party committees in highly favorable or unfavorable environments may still work to adapt. Local party organizations often think nationally but act locally, particularly after their team or brand has suffered a setback. Like sports fans who analyze reasons for team failures and earnestly debate what the team needs to do next year, party organizations—national, state, and local—look for ways to improve the party's fate come next election. The rhythm of elections, therefore, provides a strong impetus for party adaptation.

Conclusion: Local Parties in the 21st Century

Why have parties persisted so well in the United States in the face of so many seemingly fatal threats? The answer is that party organizations have been exceptionally successful at adapting to changes in the external environment. While party organizations have maintained their fundamental utility in electoral politics, the ways in which they are useful have changed. In the early 20th century, party organizations were useful both to candidates, to whom they delivered voters, and to voters, to whom they delivered jobs and services. As Progressive Era reforms undermined parties' ability to deliver goods to voters, they continued to deliver voters to candidates. As partisanship declined and mass media rose, parties adapted and found ways to deliver services to candidates who increasingly operated independently of political parties. Soft money, in particular, was a new resource that allowed parties to thrive, but even when this resource largely disappeared, parties did not wither away. Instead, they have shifted their focus from brokering money to brokering people—as we will show, local party organizations are now critical for providing labor for mobilization efforts. Across the 20th and 21st centuries, party organizations have adapted to a variety of political conditions, and it is this story of adaptation that is critical to understanding how political parties have continued to thrive over several centuries, despite a continually changing political environment. Local party organizations persist because they adapt their forms and their activities in response to a changing political environment.

The key implication of this fact is that, to have a full understanding of the role they play in American politics, local parties must be conceptualized as organizations within an environment. We need to understand how they are organized and whether organizational structure influences what they do. We need to describe what they do as organizations and whether any of this activity matters. And we need to understand how both structure and activity are shaped by the broader environment.

This environment includes the socioeconomic and political context in both the local community and in the broader state context and state party. In chapter 2, we examine the features of state political parties that vary and that may shape local political parties. State parties have a wide variety of tools they may use to shape local organizations. Whether a state party provides assistance with organization-building to local parties will surely affect that local organization's capacity to build a local party organization. Thus, we look at the nature of state party assistance to local parties and how it varies in chapter 2. Second, we believe each state party—encompassing the state committee, the local committees, and the relationships among them—has its own organizational culture that is important to understand for a full picture of the party's role in the political system. The effectiveness of this state party culture can shape the forms and activities of these local organizations. We describe the variations in party organizational culture more fully in chapter 2.

Next, in chapter 3, we examine variations in local party organizational form. Central to this understanding of local party form is organizational structure. Some local committees are highly developed institutions, with mature work routines, well-established staff positions, and relatively permanent organizational life. Other committees are moribund or dormant. Local party form, we hypothesize, is shaped by a variety of local forces, such as the socioeconomic environment and the level of interparty competition. We also believe that the assistance provided by the state party and the organizational culture of the overarching state party will affect the organizational form of local party committees in important ways.

The level of structural maturity, along with other environmental factors, determines the capacity of local party organizations to engage in electoral activity. Parties with a more mature structure will have a greater ability to engage in activity, as they will have systems in place that support undertaking these activities. Structural maturity creates capacity for action. Of course, other environmental factors—such as party competition and urbanization, to name a few—will influence the electoral activities of local parties, but we believe that parties with stronger structures will engage in more activities, a hypothesis we examine in chapter 3.

Also, we believe a party's candidates will do better when the local party is more active; after all, this is presumably why parties engage in these sorts of activities. Parties that are more active in contacting voters, organizing get-out-the-vote drives, or publicizing candidates, for example, should see payoffs in higher-than-expected vote totals for the party's candidates come election time, after controlling for other factors that influence electoral outcomes. We investigate the electoral payoff from local party activity in chapter 4.

Finally, in chapter 5 we close with a consideration of potentially emerging threats to local parties in the near future. In particular, we look at the rise of the Tea Party and what that means for local Republican party organizations. We also consider the impact that recent changes in campaign finance, in the wake of the *Citizens United* decision, mean for local party organizations.

Chapter 2

Connections and Cooperation in the State Party Confederacy

Political parties in the United States are nested organizations that work together and influence each other, but they also do not have a high degree of formal integration. State parties exist independently of the national party, and local parties operate independently of the state party. This lack of integration has caused some concern. The famous 1950 report by the APSA Committee on Political Parties, "Toward a More Responsible Two-Party System," argued forcefully for cohesive and unified parties in the United States (APSACPP 1950). The report made a case for "better integrated parties" and criticized "internal separatism," resulting from the federal structure of party organizations, as one of the basic problems facing the party system.

Almost three decades later, policymakers were similarly concerned with integrating the parties. The 1979 reforms to the Federal Election Campaign Act authorized the creation of nonfederal accounts at the party committees that could be used for party-building activities. These funds were intended to promote cooperation and assistance across party committees, primarily by allowing national parties to share money with state and local committees for general grassroots efforts and the building of organizational capacity. Of course, this purpose was later overtaken by issue advertising, earning these funds the moniker "soft money."

Despite efforts to better integrate political parties in the United States, these organizations still operate largely independently of each other. Local parties do not necessarily follow the dictates of the state and national parties; much to the chagrin of state and national party organizations, local party committees and chairs sometimes operate in ways that reflect poorly on the organization as a whole or are contrary to the wishes of those higher up in the organizational food chain. For instance, it is hard to imagine that the Republican National Committee or the North Carolina Republicans were pleased when Don Yelton, a Republican precinct committee chair in Buncombe County, stated in an interview on *The Daily Show* that voter identification laws were designed to hurt Democrats and that they may have a disproportionate impact on lazy college students and blacks.[1] To be fair, other Buncombe party officials did call for and win Yelton's resignation shortly after the interview, but he resigned because of political pressure, not because official organizational actions removed him. Local party committees and officials are independent actors in their own right. When the state party says jump, local parties don't always say how high. As Eldersveld (1964) noted, the American party system is a stratarchy, not a hierarchy. It is also accurate to think about the parties as confederacies: autonomous organizational entities that agree to cooperate in proscribed ways that do not undermine their essential independence.

That having been said, party organizations are linked together in key ways—confederation implies some coordination. As noted in the previous chapter, state regulations today encompass very specific elements of party structure in many places (Holbrook and La Raja 2013, 66). These regulations may serve to bind state and local parties more closely. Furthermore, many state party constitutions have detailed provisions about the operation of local party committees. For instance, the Massachusetts Democratic Party charter has provisions outlining the functions of local political parties, the duties of members (a minimum of 40 hours in each two-year election cycle is recommended), the number of members on town committees (no fewer than three, no more than 35), the officers in local committees, and the number of meetings per year (at least four times), among others.[2] These dictates are not always followed, as some local party committees are moribund, violating the committee membership and meeting rules, but the point remains that state political parties seek to shape the organization and operation of local political parties.

As such, while political parties in the United States are decentralized and fragmented, they are bound together in important ways. The national committees shape state parties, and the state committees influence local party organizations. The national committees have fewer ways of directly affecting local parties. The charters and rules for the DNC and RNC refer to local party committees in only a few places, mainly to set requirements for meetings and caucuses (e.g., all registered party members must be allowed to attend meetings that must be well advertised) or encourage affirmative action/nondiscrimination in membership. Local parties reside primarily in a party confederation within their states. Within these confederations, there are features of state parties and how they operate that influence the forms that local parties take and the activities they undertake. Broadly speaking, these elements of the state political party can be thought of as part of the environment that shapes the organizational forms and functions of local political parties. To be sure, there are other features of the environment, such as political competition or community demographics, that shape local political parties, and local parties are still autonomous in essential ways. But state political parties may influence these local organizations in a top-down manner.

How do state parties exert this influence? What characteristics of state parties matter? While there is some variation in the organizational form of state parties, this variation probably does not relate to the variation in forms that local party organizations take, because variation in formal structures is much smaller at the state level than at the local level. Most state political parties, even the least developed of those parties, have a state committee chair and at least a few staff. For instance, Holbrook and La Raja (2008, 64–65) note that the two major parties have state central committees headed by a state chair in all of the states and that most state parties have an executive committee that is authorized to act between meetings of the central committee. They also note that most of these organizations have permanent headquarters, professional leadership and staffing, and generous budgets (68). Even more importantly, though, it is not entirely clear how these variations would influence local party organizational form. Whether or not a state party has a treasurer probably has little impact on the way local parties do business.

However, other features of state political parties may have more influence on local party structure and activity. For instance, state parties' financial assistance to local parties probably shapes the structure and activity levels of local political parties, as money can be used to rent offices, hire part-time staff, or pay for a telephone listing. Money can also be used to buy advertising or put on fundraising events. Thus, assistance from state political parties may induce organizational adaptation at the local level. As Gibson et al. (1989, 69) note in talking about state party assistance, "Norms and incentives emanating from these organizations strongly encourage local parties to develop organizational and technical solutions to their political problems." This is the sort of top-down organizational adaptation described in chapter 1; state political parties can strategically provide assistance to local parties to foster adaptation.

Furthermore, as with other organizations, political parties have unique organizational cultures, which are shared across the state political environment. Organizational cultures encompass shared mental assumptions and values that guide action in organizations and that help define appropriate behavior in various situations (Ravasi and Shultz 2006). Importantly, these cultures give rise to a set of management practices or activities that are rooted in these values of the organization (Denison 1990). As Robbins (2005) notes, a shared organizational culture can serve as a control mechanism that guides the behaviors of members of the organization. As a result, the organizational culture of political parties may influence the shape and activities of local party organizations. For instance, state party organizational cultures that value innovation may produce local parties that are better at adapting to the local political environment.

In this chapter, we examine two important features of state political parties that shape the organizational form of local parties: the amount and type of assistance that state parties offer to local parties and the organizational culture of state parties. As we will show in this chapter, there are variations in both the amount of assistance offered and the culture of state parties that are shaped by the state political environment. In chapter 3, we will look at how these factors shape local party structure and activity.

Survey of Local Party Chairs

If assistance from state party organizations influences local party form, then we need to know the level and types of assistance state parties are providing to these local parties. To gather these data, and other data used throughout the book, we conducted a survey of local party chairs in the United States in 2010. These surveys asked the local party chairs to reflect on their organization's structure and activity levels, as well as some aspects of the state party organization and activities.[3] In addition to the survey, follow-up telephone interviews were conducted with a handful of the respondents.

To start, efforts were made to secure email addresses for all local party chairs in all states from state party websites and officials. In almost all states, these local party committees are organized at the county level. In some states, particularly in the Northeast, town committees are either the additional or primary unit, and in some states (North Dakota, Alaska), state legislative districts serve as the main jurisdiction for local committees. Most state political parties provided lists of email addresses for the local parties on the state party website. In other states, state party officials were willing to share a list directly. Not all parties posted or shared their local party email addresses, and even when they did there were frequently some addresses that were unavailable. Many addresses turned out to be nonworking and, of course, there were many officials who refused or simply chose not to take the survey online.

In the end, invitations to participate were sent to 4,342 party officials. Email addresses for Democratic officials were located in 47 states and for Republican officials in 41 states (in only one state, Missouri, were no addresses obtained for either party). Of course, in some states only a handful of addresses could be ascertained, while in others addresses were numerous and available. This variation reflects both the willingness of the state party to share the email addresses as well as the number of counties, towns, or districts within the state that are the seat for local party organizations. Three waves of survey invitations were sent during April through August 2010.

There were 1,220 responses, 544 from Republicans and 676 from Democrats. Responses were received from local chairs in 86 state parties (46 from Democratic and 40 from Republican parties). The number of responses varies considerably from state to state as shown in table A.1 in the appendix, reflecting the variation in the number of local committees, the number of email addresses available, and the response rates. After collecting responses, we determined that some respondents were not chairs but filled other roles within the party organizations, such as other officers or poll watchers. This was the case for 10 Republican respondents in Alaska and 23 Republican respondents in Massachusetts. These respondents are excluded in the main analyses in the book, for which the local party committee is the unit of analysis. Thus, the actual number of local chair responses is 1,187, with 511 Republicans and 676 Democrats. The nonchair responses, however, were utilized in the construction of the state party organizational culture measures, which we discuss later.

To assess the representativeness of the sample, we can compare the demographic makeup of the counties that responded to this survey with all counties in the United States; this is not a perfect comparison, since some local parties fall into town or district jurisdictions, but it provides a good approximation. An analysis of the data reveals the sample covers populations that are more urbanized, wealthier, more educated, and more supportive of Democratic presidential candidates than the average county in the United States. The comparisons of the sample averages versus the full population averages are as follows: percent urbanized, 52% versus 40%; median household income, $52,000 versus $44,000; percent with bachelor's or higher, 24% versus 19%; percent voting for Obama, 45% versus 42%.

Because the first three of these variables correlate positively with both structure and activity, this bias suggests structure and activity levels in the sample will be higher than the full population. This is not surprising:

moribund parties are less likely to have a chair engaged enough to respond to a survey request. Cotter et al. (1984) take the approach of simply adding an arbitrary number of inactive committees to their sample. We do not think such an approach is justified here for several reasons. First, our sample does contain a significant number of responses from organizations that did not engage in any activities in the 2008 election campaign—in fact, 4% of the local chairs reported no activity. So, the sample has not excluded dormant committees. Second, absent information on the true distribution of structure and activity in the population, we cannot simply assume that nonresponse is due to inactivity. As such, we do not try to correct for this in our sample. So, some degree of caution is in order as structure and activity levels in the data must be considered high-end estimates. That said, the socioeconomic bias is not likely to have large effects on sampled structure and activity levels, for the simple reason that socioeconomics are not that strongly predictive of structure and activity. As a set, the three socioeconomic variables explain only 17% of the variation in overall structural maturity and only 6% of overall activity levels (we examine these relationships more fully in chapter 3). Given that we have counties in our sample that represent a broad range of demographic (high and low socioeconomic status, rural and urban) and organizational (engaged in many activities and engaged in none) characteristics, we feel confident we have sufficient variation to allow us to draw valid conclusions about local parties in the United States.

To measure local party structure, activity and state assistance, we utilize the same set of survey items originally used in the Party Transformation Study (PTS) from 1980 (Cotter et al. 1984) and later in the Election Dynamics Project (EDP) conducted in the 1990s by Frendreis and Gitelson (1999). The full text of the survey is located in the appendix. In addition to the common items, there were several new questions, mainly relating to email, website, and social media usage. For all of these questions, respondents were asked to report whether their local party had a particular structural trait or engaged in a specific activity in the most recent election. There was also an additional battery of questions designed to measure state party organizational culture, which we discuss in greater length later in this chapter.

When examining local party structure and activity, the unit of analysis is the local party committee, and care must be taken when making inferences from a group of local parties to what is representative of all local parties in a state. While the number of respondents for some states is quite large, in many states the number of respondents from each party is relatively small. In only a few states are there enough respondents to have confidence that the structure and activity of the sample can be inferred to the population of all local parties in the state. As a result, we do not attempt to aggregate to the state level based on local party responses, at least in terms of parameters that require a statistical inference from sample to population. For these inferences, we aggregate only to the national level.

Assistance from the State Party

As part of our survey of local parties, we asked local party chairs a variety of questions about what kind of assistance they received from the state party in the 2008 election cycle. We asked local party chairs if they had received any of the following kinds of assistance from the state party: financial record keeping, legal advice, computer services, research office space, staff assistance with candidate recruitment, funds for operating expenses, funds for campaign expenses, campaign training and schools, web development, and social media assistance. Using these data, we can examine the extent to which state party assistance varies both across the political parties as well as how it varies within the political parties.

Looking at the individual activities and types of assistance by party as shown in figure 2.1 (pg. 30), there are some areas where local parties and state parties have relatively low levels of interaction. For instance, few state parties assisted local parties with campaign expenses, operating expenses, office space, or staff. Fewer than 15% of local party organizations reported receiving any of these types of assistance. As a result, we might expect few local political parties will have paid staff and year-round operations. However, it is interesting that state parties are not providing much support for campaign expenses, given that the primary function of US political parties is electoral in nature. It may be that this type of support is going directly to candidates, so local parties are more likely to engage in other sorts of activities. The low levels of financial assistance to local parties may also reflect the aftermath of BCRA. Research has shown that state political parties shifted away from money-intensive activities after the passage of BCRA (Dwyre et al. 2007; La Raja, Orr, and Smith 2006). Compared to the levels of assistance with campaign expenses in the 1980s, there have been statistically significant declines among both Democrats and Republicans (Roscoe and Jenkins 2014).

At the high end, over 60% of local party organizations report receiving campaign training from the state political party, both for Democrats and Republicans. It is hard to reconcile this finding with the previous finding

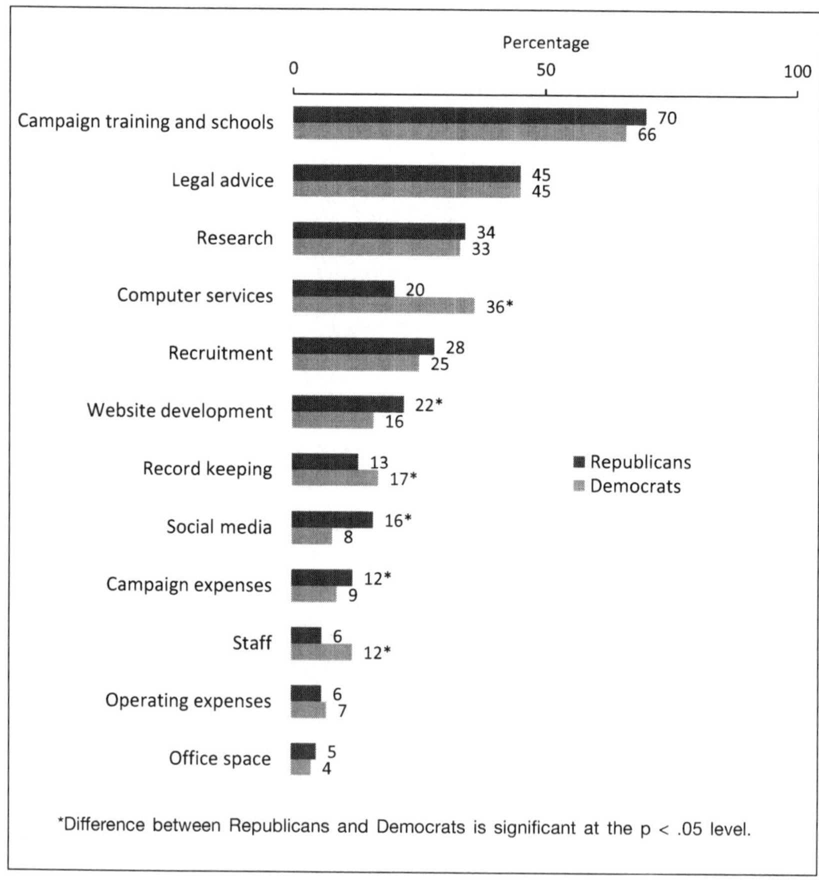

FIGURE 2.1. The Percentage of Local Parties Receiving Assistance from State Party

because it would seem that campaign expenses and training would go hand in hand. But taken together, these results seem to confirm at the local level what research has found at the state level. State parties are shifting from money-intensive activities to labor intensive activities (Dwyre et al. 2007; La Raja et al. 2007). To the extent that people are the key resource that local parties marshal come election time and given that it is difficult for state parties to control local party organizations, it may be that campaign training assistance is a way to professionalize and shape local party activists. Furthermore, such training activities ensure there are well-trained, ready-to-go boots on the ground come election season. We discuss these considerations more fully in chapter 5.

There are some significant differences between the Democrats and the Republicans in terms of the assistance they provide to local party organizations. State Democratic parties are significantly more likely to provide local parties with computer assistance, record keeping, and staff assistance, but Republican state parties are significantly more likely to help with campaign expenses. Also, Republican state parties are more likely to help with both internet functions (website development and social media). However, there are generally similar patterns for both parties overall. Both parties are most likely to provide their local organizations with assistance with campaign training and legal advice. The least common forms of assistance are staff, financial record keeping, operating expenses, and office space. Web development and social media assistance are relatively uncommon, too, although it is probably best to consider these as emergent forms of activity during this time period.

Factor analysis also indicates that certain types of assistance are more likely to be delivered together, as table 2.1 indicates. This factor analysis,

Table 2.1. State Party Assistance: Rotated Factor Loadings

	Core Assistance Factor	Special Assistance Factor	Expenses Assistance Factor	Internet Assistance Factor
Office Space	0.4005	0.1125	0.2066	0.0350
Staff	0.3983	0.1520	0.2416	0.0289
Financial Records	0.0552	0.2948	0.1166	0.1476
Legal	0.0406	0.5375	0.0476	0.1176
Computer	0.1633	0.3340	0.0926	0.1758
Research	0.1148	0.5534	0.1473	0.1257
Candidate Recruitment	0.0879	0.3634	0.1650	0.1563
Campaign Training	0.0408	0.4624	0.0070	0.1914
Campaign Expenses	0.0865	0.1223	0.4786	0.0904
Operating Expenses	0.1708	0.0758	0.4868	0.0947
Social Media	0.0031	0.1377	0.0953	0.5059
Web Development	0.0451	0.1834	0.0638	0.5333

which utilized varimax rotation, suggested four factors among the data (both the AIC and the BIC statistics were minimized at four factors). Office space and staff load onto the Core Assistance factor.[4] Staff and space are "core" in the sense that they provide organizational capacity to engage in almost any kind of activity. Also, renting out office space or hiring personnel would seem to require some sort of longer-term commitment that is not present in the other types of assistance. Core assistance would likely be delivered as an ongoing subsidy, if at all. For example, a local party chair in Maine described a relatively formalized "partnership program," in which the state party provided office space as well as paid, coordinated campaign staff. Financial record keeping, legal, computer, research, recruitment, and training all load onto a second factor, which we term Special Assistance. These types of assistance share two key characteristics. First, they involve the sharing of expertise; local parties may not have the resources or connections to engage this sort of expertise, but state party organizations, which tend to be fairly professional, may have people on staff who can provide this knowledge, or the state party may have financial resources to purchase it. In this regard, it is notable that the items in this factor are the most frequent forms of assistance (see figure 2.1). Second, these commitments are not necessarily ongoing. State parties may provide occasional legal expertise or hold annual training sessions, but this does not necessarily mean they need to provide this support every month or even every year—they can provide it on an as-needed (or as-can-afford) basis.

Assistance with operating expenses and campaign expenses load onto the third factor, Expenses Assistance. This factor is clearly about money; when state parties have it, they provide it both to build local parties and to run campaigns. A fourth factor is termed Internet Assistance; website development and social media assistance load here. The factor analysis suggests some state parties are more focused on developing these capacities at the local level than others.

Cumulatively, most local party organizations are receiving some sort of assistance from the state party, as shown in figure 2.2. Local parties, on average, receive close to three kinds of assistance from the state party (2.77 on average across all local parties). The distribution for assistance from the state party is somewhat positively skewed. Very few organizations reported they have received all 12 forms of assistance from their state party, but it was also uncommon for local parties to report they had received no assistance, with just over 16% selecting this option. Most commonly, local parties received one to four types of assistance from the state party.

Furthermore, there appears to be little difference between the parties in terms of the cumulative assistance they offer to local party organizations, as figure 2.2 shows; the distribution of assistance is not substantially different between the two parties. The mean for Democrats and Republicans is identical (2.77), and the standard deviation nearly so (2.19 vs. 2.23). So while there are some significant differences between the parties in terms of the types of assistance they provide to local party organizations, the total amount of assistance provided to local parties is remarkably similar.

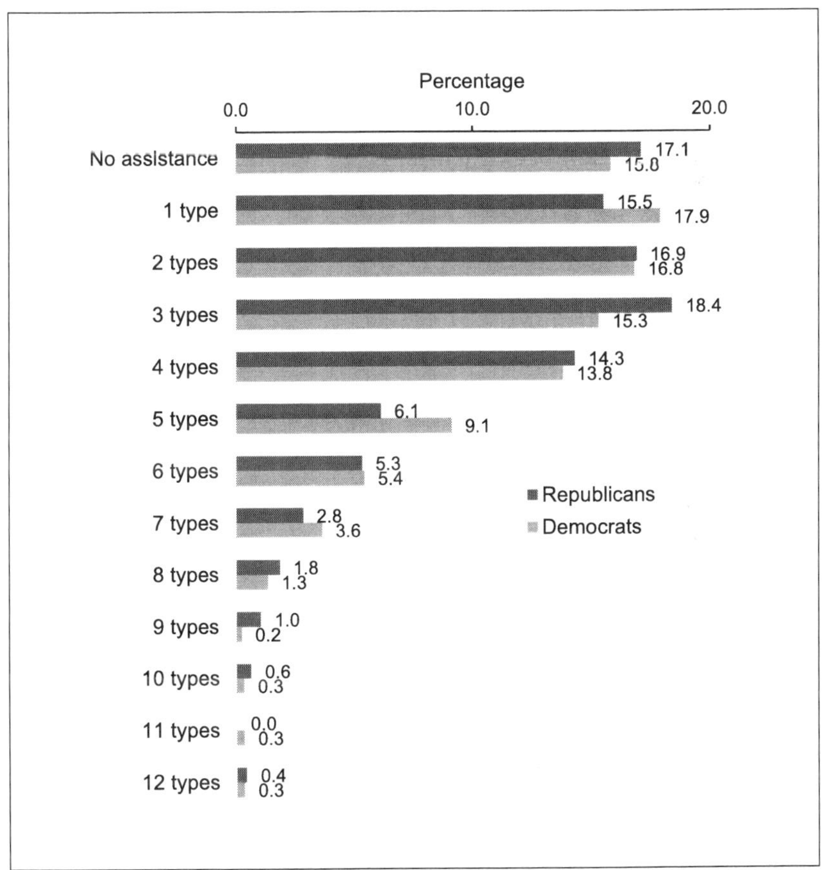

FIGURE 2.2. The Frequency of Different Levels of Assistance to Local Parties from State Parties

To say the Democrats and Republicans do not differ greatly in the total amount of assistance they provide does not imply there is little variation in assistance. First, as we noted earlier, the two parties differ some in the types of assistance they provide. But, also, there is variation across the 100 state parties in the amount of assistance they provide, and more importantly, there is considerable variation *within* individual state party organizations in terms of their assistance to individual local party committees. A simple ANOVA reveals 86% of the variation in overall assistance received by local parties falls within state parties and only 14% falls between them. In other words, state parties discriminate among their local committees in terms of whom to support with assistance. Similar patterns are evident across all four assistance factors, with 81% of the variation in Core Assistance, 87% of the variation in Special Assistance, 82% of the variation in Expenses Assistance, and 86% of the variation in Internet Assistance falling within state parties.

Moreover, the standard deviation varies considerably across the states. In other words, some state parties provide fairly equal assistance to all their local parties, while others favor some local organizations over others. This pattern is illustrated in figure 2.3, which displays the standard deviation in assistance levels by parties across the states.[5] High standard deviations suggest the state party is giving lots of assistance to some local parties and little to others; lower standard deviations imply a more equitable distribution. Looking first at the Democratic Party, the average on this measure across the states is 2.1; at the high end is Minnesota, with a standard deviation of 3.1, and at the low end is California, with a standard deviation of 1.5; California actually has a higher average level of assistance (3.3) as compared to Minnesota (1.9), which suggests that the variation in assistance is not necessarily related to the average level of assistance. So within the Democratic Party, some state parties are giving very different levels of assistance to different local political parties, while other state parties are distributing this assistance more evenly.

The same is true of Republican Party assistance, as figure 2.3 shows. Here, Illinois has the highest standard deviation at 2.9, while Tennessee scores the lowest, at 1.4. For the Republicans, the mean amount of assistance across these two state parties is very similar (2.9 versus 2.7, respectively), again demonstrating that average assistance levels are not necessarily tied to the variation in assistance levels. Thus, assistance to local parties varies not just by party but by state within those parties as well.

Unfortunately, the nature of our data does not allow us to fully model this variation because we do not have representative samples within each state. However, our data suggest this may be driven partly by the

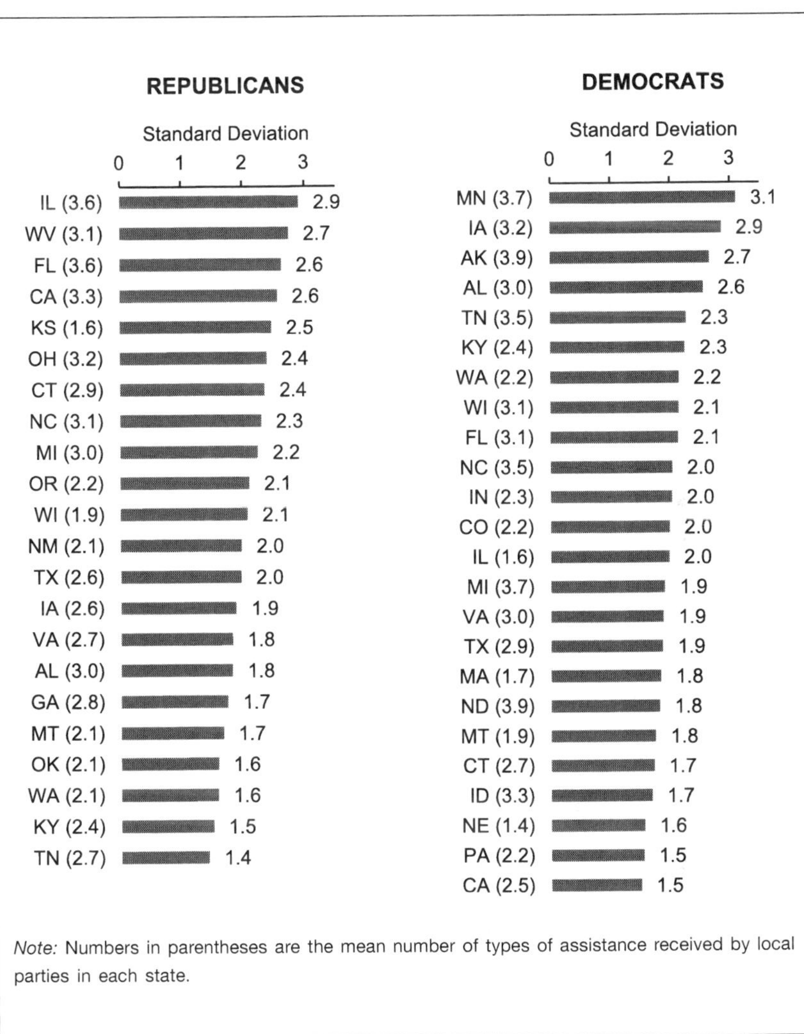

Note: Numbers in parentheses are the mean number of types of assistance received by local parties in each state.

FIGURE 2.3. Standard Deviation of Total State Party Assistance within State Parties

characteristics of the counties themselves (Jenkins and Roscoe 2011). For instance, state party assistance for Democratic parties is negatively related to county urbanization. This may seem counterintuitive at first but may reflect two factors. First, Democratic parties may see urban counties as "in the bag" and so not worthy of additional assistance. Second, these urban counties may not need assistance from the state. For example, the Cook County Democratic party probably has resources that rival those of the Illinois state Democratic party, so Cook County may not ask for help, or the state party may allocate resources to counties with fewer of their own resources. Other county-level variables, such as county-level competition, population, or median household income, are not significantly related to state party assistance, though.

Patterns of assistance may also be driven partly by relationships between county and state party officials. A Democratic chair of a Florida county party explained that state party officials there are more inclined to provide assistance to people they know and with whom they have relationships, even as they believe the distribution of assistance is purely strategic. Similarly, a local South Carolina chair complained that the state Democratic party officials tended to help out local candidates and parties with whom they had a personal connection; there was a sense that they were courting favor with the political establishment in the state. These dynamics may undermine the effectiveness of this assistance. Local Democratic chairs in both South Carolina and Georgia felt state assistance was targeted significantly to counties with competitive state races, with perhaps not enough aid going to places with competitive congressional contests. These impressions suggest some areas of more systematic analysis. To the extent that state party assistance drives the form and activities of local political parties—and as we show in chapter 3, it does—then understanding why this assistance varies is an important future research question.

Overall, the picture of state and local party integration would not satisfy those who advocate for responsible parties. On the other hand, political parties are not totally disintegrated in the United States. Most local parties, both on the Democratic and Republican sides, report receiving some form of state assistance, such that we can say there is some level of attachment and integration between state and local party organizations. State party organizations are actively providing assistance to local political parties. The level and types of assistance vary both between parties and, particularly, within parties across the states. And the assistance state parties provide tends to come in certain packages, such as technological outreach or money. Thus, assistance from the state party, whether it comes in the form of campaign training, office space, or something else, may play a role in local party adaptation because different types and levels of assistance may induce different types of organizational forms. The extent to which assistance to local parties from state parties exerts a top-down influence on local parties' structure and activity is a question we turn to in chapter 3. For now, we look at the other key way state parties may shape local party structure and activity: organizational culture.

Political Party Organizational Culture

For several decades, students of corporate management have studied the organizational culture of business firms as a way to understand the effectiveness of firms and the ways in which individual behavior is shaped by collective values. However, organizational culture has not been widely studied in political science, especially in the context of American political organizations. This failure is particularly unfortunate, because American parties seem to display clearly distinctive cultures in the broader sense of the term (see Bernstein, Bromley, and Meyer 2006).[6] Freeman's (1986) description of the cultures of the Democratic and Republican parties is perhaps one of the only studies that attempts to document these differences, but her data is primarily descriptive and is limited to only looking at the national parties, as opposed to examining how and why culture varies within the many party organizations and whether this matters.

The widespread use of the red state/blue state distinction is at least partly due to the fact that it signifies to us much more than voting tendencies. Because the parties embody distinct cultural norms and values, it would be surprising if these broader cultural values were not reflected in the *organizational* cultures of the Democratic and Republican parties as well. Differences in the cultures and histories of individual states might also shape the kinds of party organizational cultures that emerge. Given the extensive literature in organizational theory demonstrating a link between culture and behavior, it would also be surprising if this culture did not shape how parties organize and operate. In the state party confederacies, these cultures should shape what happens at the local level. What do we mean, then, by organizational culture, and how do we think it will operate in political parties?

We can start by looking at contemporary research on organizational culture. This concept has its roots in two literatures: the largely ethnographic studies of organizational culture and the more quantitative literature focusing on organizational "climate" (see Denison 1996 for a review of these literatures). Despite their differing epistemological and methodological approaches, Denison (1996, 625) argues that both define organizational culture as "the internal social psychological environment of organizations and the relationship of that environment to individual meaning and organizational adaptation."

In both approaches, culture is captured by a set of core values or "shared basic assumptions" (Schein 1992; Trice and Beyer 1993). Whether these values are discovered through ethnographic field observation or quantitative survey analysis, they provide researchers with a way to understand the collective properties of an organization and how these properties shape, and are shaped by, the individuals inhabiting those organizations.

In contemporary studies, the approach is generally reliant on survey data, but researchers have embraced the label "culture" and have grounded their theories in the older organizational culture literature as well as the climate literature (Chatman 1989; Chatman 1991; Denison 1990; Hofstede et al. 1990; O'Reilly, Chatman, and Caldwell 1991; Rousseau 1990). Typically, researchers identify a set of value or trait statements and ask respondents to indicate the extent to which these typify the organization's culture. Commonly, these data are reduced to a small set of cultural dimensions. So measured, culture has been used to study selection and socialization processes (Chatman 1991), person-organization fit and its relationship to individual behavior (Chatman 1989; O'Reilly, Chatman, and Caldwell 1991), and organizational effectiveness (Denison 1990).

Though the study of organizational culture has focused primarily on business firms, political parties almost certainly have their own organizational cultures. A party organization is clearly different from business firms in important ways, but it shares with firms two needs that generate culture: internal integration and external adaptation (see Schein 1992). As discussed in chapter 1, the need to adapt to a changing external environment has been nearly constant for American parties. And while political parties are not nearly as tightly integrated as businesses, the lack of formal control mechanisms between different levels of party organizations makes the need for internal integration even greater.

Applying the concept of culture to parties, however, requires some modification to the theories developed in the management literature. For example, the boundaries of the group are less clear. In a firm, the organization comprises the employees. But what are the boundaries of the party organization? Clearly, the party officials would be included, but what about their staff? Would state and county party officials be part of a single organization? What about the party-in-government? These individuals are, at least in some respects, distinct from party officials but at the same time are part of the same group.

Also, the culture literature often discusses the importance of recruitment and selection in maintaining an organization's cultural identity. But parties, both organizationally and legislatively, do not hire and fire in the way corporations do. As we noted in chapter 1, parties are highly permeable. At the same time, identification with, and commitment to, a party is often grounded in basic ideological congruence. As a result, party members typically agree on a wide range of political values. This agreement is likely to have effects on culture that are not evident in the business world.

To measure organizational culture with our survey of local party chairs, we examined many of the most widely used instruments in the organizational culture literature, including those by Post, de Coning, and Smit (1997); Cameron and Quinn (1999); O'Reilly, Chatman, and Caldwell (1991); Denison (1990); and others. We drew and adapted from these what was most applicable to the study of parties and added additional questions to address unique areas of party culture. Because the study of corporate culture is often tied to evaluating the effectiveness of the firm or understanding why some firms are successful, many of the survey instruments assess traits that most would agree take on a clear positive/negative connotation. For instance, Post, de Coning, and Smit (1997) measure a dimension labeled "goal clarity," which they define as the "degree to which the organization creates clear objectives and performance expectations" (149). In this case, higher scores can clearly be interpreted as "better" insofar as they are likely to lead to a more effective and successful organization. This perspective might be thought of as an evaluative understanding of organizational culture. In contrast, O'Reilly, Chatman, and Caldwell (1991) uncover a factor they label "team orientation." For some firms in certain contexts, a team orientation may be adaptive and effective, but in others a more individualistic and competitive culture may be more successful. These kinds of cultural traits represent alternative norms and styles of organization, but their presence cannot be said to be positive or negative without understanding the context and challenges of the organization.

For our purposes here, we focus on the evaluative conceptualization of culture. We identify seven *cultural attributes* that represent positive qualities of organizations; parties that score highly on these measures should function more effectively:

Culture management: extent to which party works to create
shared culture
Innovativeness: extent to which party responds to external
environment

> *Strategic clarity:* extent to which party clearly defines goals
> *Organizational focus:* extent to which party focuses on central mission
> *Horizontal integration:* extent to which information is shared
> *Reward orientation:* extent to which performance is rewarded
> *Identification with the organization:* extent to which members feel committed to party

Local party chairs in our survey were asked to identify the organizational culture of their state party through a series of questions. Each attribute has several survey items that contribute to the attribute score; the appendix has a full description of the items used for each attribute. Each item has a 1 to 5 scale, and each attribute score represents the means of the items, so each attribute runs 1 to 5. Our measurements proceed on the assumption that the important party culture to examine is the one operating at the state level. Local parties may have their own unique organizational cultures, though many may not, insofar as there is often little "organization" beyond the chair and perhaps a few other activists. This makes it difficult to assess organizational culture at the local level. Some county parties, perhaps those in urban areas or in places where a particular party is advantaged, may have a developed organization with distinct cultural norms, but other county parties, such as those in rural areas where a particular party is disadvantaged, may not be developed enough to see the development of a unique county organizational culture. For instance, the Cook County Democrats may have their own unique organizational culture, but the Hampshire Republican party in western Massachusetts probably does not. As a result, county organizational culture is inconsistently developed across local counties. But as noted earlier, nearly all state parties are relatively well developed at this point in time (Holbrook and La Raja 2013), such that organizational culture can develop at the state level. Thus, we are interested in the broader set of norms and organizational practices that overarch all of these local parties at the state level—the organizational culture of the entire state party confederacy. This culture results from the unique history of the party in that state and the ideas and practices of its leaders over time. It has evolved over time in response to key environmental pressures. To the extent that county parties interact regularly with the state party (and they do, as previously demonstrated), state party organizational culture infuses party activity and behavior at all levels within the state. As a result, our measurement relies on local party chairs to describe this state organizational culture rather than what they perceive to be unique to their locality.[7]

Cultural Differences between Democrats and Republicans

To start, we can examine the differences between the organizational culture of the Democrats and Republicans overall. Though we expect variation among the various state parties, are there also differences at this highest level of aggregation? Figure 2.4 (pg. 42) displays the average score on each of the attributes for the two parties, which is to say the averages for the 46 Republican state parties and the 40 Democratic state parties.[8] Across all attributes, the Republicans display higher averages than the Democrats, although not all of these differences are statistically significant. For five of the seven attributes, the differences between the parties are around .1. This is somewhat remarkable as other research has found distinct differences in other aspects of party cultures, such as the political beliefs and popular culture preferences (Bernstein, Bromley, and Meyer 2006; Freeman 1986). For instance, Freeman argues, based on observational data, that Democrats are more apt to identify with constituencies within the party, whereas Republicans are much more homogenous and firmly attached to the party. However, our data, which focus on the management of the party as an organization, do not support this as there is no significant difference between the Democrats and Republicans in terms of their identification with the party. In fact, the paucity of significant differences suggests that electoral pressures induce parties to become more effective, generally speaking. Just as the old saying suggests "there isn't a Democratic or Republican way to pave a street," it may be that there is no distinctly Democratic or Republican way to run a party organization. Instead, parties generally develop and adapt their organization in response to the environment in which they reside. Furthermore, it is important to remember that attributes represent positive qualities of effective organizations. Electoral pressures appear to induce parties to become effective, as all of the average scores for the parties are close to the more effective end of the scale of measurement, which leads to remarkable similarities between the Democrats and the Republicans in the aggregate.

However, there are some differences between the parties on these measures of organizational culture. The Republicans have significantly higher scores on the culture management and strategic clarity attributes, which seems to be a bit more consistent with Freeman's (1986) notion that Republicans are more focused on the organization as a whole. It is important to note, though, that these differences are generally not large (.1 or .2 on a five-point scale), although the Republicans' score on the strategic clarity attribute is .37 points higher than the Democratic score. Taken together, these results suggest the Republicans have a slight edge over Democrats in

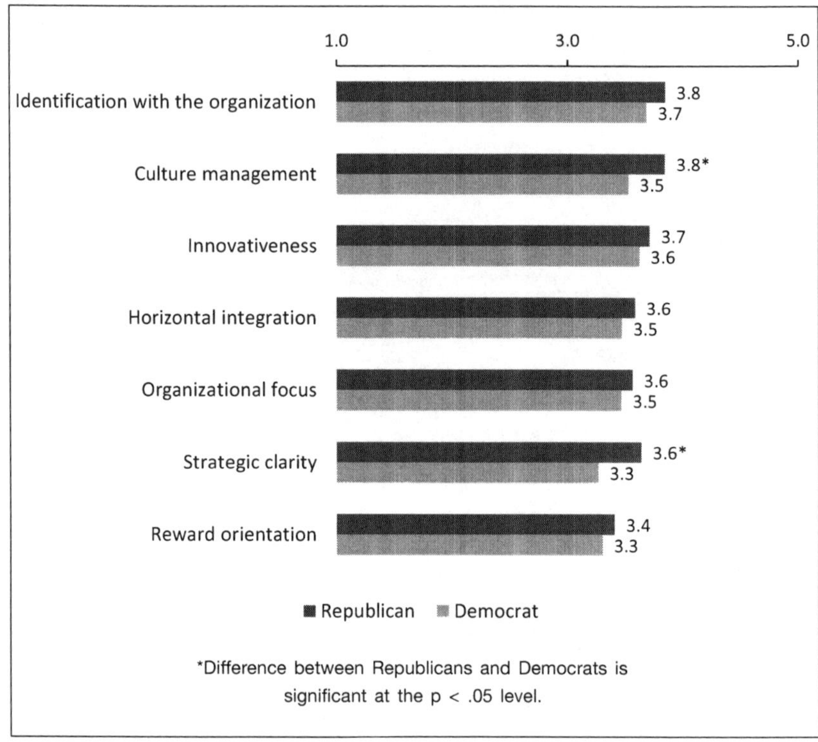

FIGURE 2.4. Average Party Organizational Culture Attribute Scores for Democrats and Republicans

creating a more effective organizational culture, although both parties seem to have gravitated toward creating efficient and effective organizations.

Factor analysis reveals that all of the attributes load very strongly on one factor; a second factor is plausible, given the values for some of the various selection criteria, but an examination of this factor suggests it is only mildly distinguishable from the first (even after varimax rotation).[9] In other words, all seven attributes load strongly on both factors, with some loading just a bit more strongly on one or the other. The patterns of these loadings, however, do not suggest any obvious connections among the attributes that load higher on either factor. For these reasons, we conclude that the attributes all contribute to a single underlying dimension: organizational culture effectiveness.

Cultural Difference within Parties and States

Of course, we are interested here in examining not just the cultures of the two parties overall but also how this culture varies across the specific state parties. The data reveal there is indeed considerable variation across the state parties on these measures. To take one example, figure 2.5 (pg. 44) shows each state party's score on the culture management attribute. These scores range from a high of 4.7 in Delaware to a low of 1.7 in Nevada, a three-point difference on a five-point scale. These across-party differences are not confined to the Republicans. Democratic scores on the culture management attribute range from a high of 4.4 in Mississippi to a low of 2.7 in New York.

This variation in cultural effectiveness is not limited to culture management. Table 2.2 provides the range and standard deviation for all of the attributes across all the state parties, calculated separately for Democrats and Republicans. Each party shows considerable range on these measures, with relatively large differences between the minimum and maximum values. However, the dispersion is only moderate—for both parties, the standard deviation is always below .5 on a five-point scale. Nonetheless, there are some interesting patterns in the data. Generally speaking, the Republicans tend to have less variation on these measures than the Democrats.

Table 2.2. Range and Standard Deviation of Party Organizational Cultural Attributes

	Republicans			Democrats		
	Min.	Max.	Std. Dev.	Min.	Max.	Std. Dev.
Culture Management	2.7	4.4	0.4	1.7	4.7	0.5
Innovativeness	2.8	4.3	0.3	2.7	4.7	0.4
Strategic Clarity	2.6	4.6	0.4	2.3	4.1	0.4
Organizational Focus	2.7	4.2	0.4	2.7	4.7	0.4
Horizontal Integration	2.3	4.5	0.4	2.3	5.0	0.4
Reward Orientation	2.5	4.1	0.3	2.3	5.0	0.4
Identification with Organization	2.5	4.5	0.4	2.4	4.7	0.4

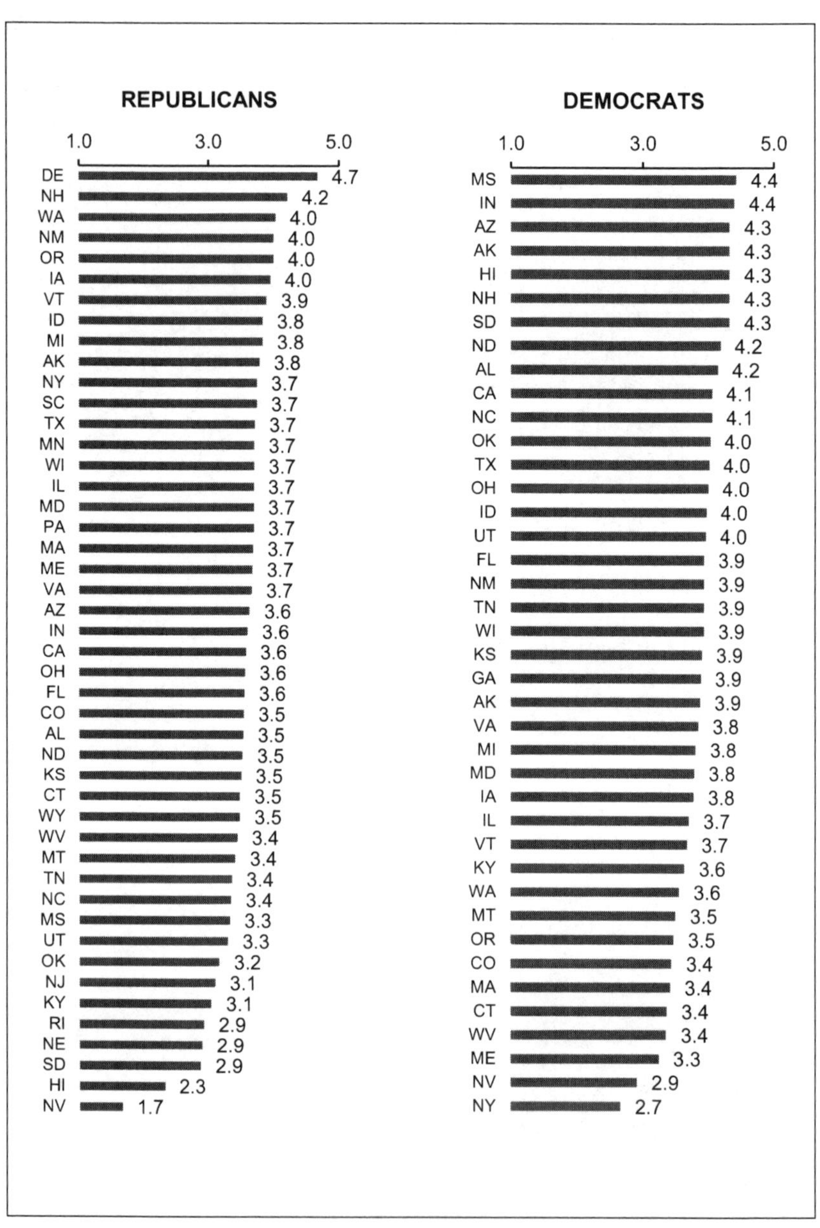

FIGURE 2.5. Party Organizational Culture Management Scores by State Party

Since attributes are a measure of cultural effectiveness (with high scores representing more effective cultures), we can also examine the high and low scores on these measures to understand where the most and least effective cultures are located. Table 2.3 (pg. 46) presents the high- and low-scoring state parties on each attribute. In the Democratic Party, New Hampshire, Delaware, and New Mexico appear the most times in the states with the highest average score for each attribute, with six, four, and three mentions, respectively. On the low end, Hawaii, Nevada, and South Dakota appear multiple times among the low scores for Democrats (three, four, and four times, respectively).

For the Republicans, New Hampshire, with six mentions, stands out as having an effective culture, although several other states (Hawaii, Mississippi, and North Dakota) appear more than once on the list. On the low side for Republicans, only four states appear on the low-scoring list: Maine, Nevada, New Mexico, and New York. For both Democrats and Republicans, New Hampshire stands out as a state that has effective party cultures across both sides of the aisle. It ranks in the top three on six attributes for both the Democrats and the Republicans. Perhaps New Hampshire's early primary produces a particularly effective organizational culture, although if this were the case, one would expect Iowa to show up here as well. Conversely, Nevada stands out as having particularly ineffective cultures despite its early primary date, appearing among the low scores four times for the Democrats and seven times for the Republicans. The factors driving these variations in culture are presumably complex and beyond the scope of this book, but the important point here is that these organizational cultures do vary—by party and by state within those parties. As with state party assistance, the interesting question, to which we turn in the next chapter, is the extent to which these cultural differences matter for the form and activity levels of local party organizations.

Conclusion: State Party Influence on Local Parties

We started this chapter with the premise that, while political parties in the United States are decentralized and fragmented, they are bound together in important ways. These ties that bind parties across levels of the organization mean there is potential for influence across levels. While the national party surely has some influence over state parties, our focus here has been on the ways that state parties may shape the organization and activities of

Table 2.3. States with High and Low Party Organizational Culture Attribute Scores

	Democrats High	Democrats Low	Republicans High	Republicans Low
Culture Management	Delaware	Nevada	Mississippi	New York
	New Hampshire	Hawaii	Indiana	Nevada
	Washington	South Dakota	New Hampshire	Maine
Innovativeness	Delaware	Maine	New Hampshire	New York
	New Hampshire	South Dakota	Indiana	Nevada
	West Virginia	Kentucky	Utah	Maine
Strategic Clarity	New Hampshire	Nevada	New Hampshire	Nevada
	Washington	Hawaii	Hawaii	New York
	Iowa	Nebraska	Arkansas	New Mexico
Organizational Focus	Delaware	Maine	South Dakota	Maine
	New Hampshire	South Dakota	Arkansas	New Mexico
	New Mexico	Nebraska	Mississippi	New York
Horizontal Integration	Delaware	Rhode Island	New Hampshire	New York
	New Hampshire	Indiana	North Dakota	Nevada
	Idaho	South Dakota	Mississippi	Maine
Reward Orientation	Delaware	Nevada	New Hampshire	New York
	New Hampshire	Kentucky	Arizona	Nevada
	New Mexico	New Jersey	Alabama	New Mexico
Identification with Organization	Delaware	Hawaii	New Hampshire	New York
	New Mexico	Nevada	Hawaii	Nevada
	New Hampshire	Nebraska	North Dakota	New Mexico

local parties. These state party influences can be thought of as part of the environment that shapes the organizational forms and functions of local political parties. These influences compete and work with other potential influences, such as the local socioeconomic and political context in which the local party resides, to shape how a local party adapts.

The analysis presented here demonstrates that there is considerable variation across the parties and within the parties on two key features of state parties that we believe shape local parties: assistance and culture. Some state parties provide more assistance, some less. Some state parties provide this assistance more uniformly to local parties, while other state parties target their assistance. Organizational culture also varies across the parties and across the states. Some state parties have more effective organizational cultures, some less. And while Republicans generally have a more effective culture than the Democrats overall, the considerable variation at the state level means that some state Republican parties have less effective political cultures than their Democratic counterparts. Whether and how these two factors influence local political parties is the question we turn to next.

Of course, assistance can be used to build organizations, and culture is a unifying force across the levels of political parties, but there is still considerable independence at the local level, even in parties that value centralization and hierarchy. This means that there is much variation in local party committees. Some may be highly organized and structurally mature, others less so. Some local parties may be highly active, despite lacking assistance from the state party organization. But these factors, structural maturity and activity levels, represent the fundamentals of organizational form, and they serve as key markers describing the vitality and functional role of local party organizations. We next turn to how and why these features of local committees vary.

Organizational Structure and Activity at the Local Level

In 2008, local parties geared up for the presidential election, organizing and working on behalf of the party and its candidates. But across the country, the vigor with which these local party committees organized and worked varied. For instance, one local Democratic committee in Nebraska was largely devoid of any organizational structure or activity; it reported having no staff, office, or internet presence, nor did it engage in any electoral activities, such as distributing campaign signs or organizing door-to-door canvassing. However, another local Democratic committee in the same state reported having a fully developed local committee, with paid staff, a year-round office, and a telephone listing. It also reported engaging in telephone campaigns, get-out-the-vote drives, and billboard advertising. These two parties reside in similar state political environments, with vastly different structure and activity levels. Based on this, one might conclude that the state political environment is irrelevant. However, there are also clear patterns in activity levels by state; for example, local Idaho Republican organizations reported engaging in eight electoral activities on average in 2008, while local Indiana Republican organizations reported engaging in over fifteen activities on average.

Looking across our data, we see active and inactive Democratic and Republican committees; some of these organizations are structurally robust, while others are active with bare-bones organizational structure. We see this variation within states and across states. These organizations are remarkably different in what they look like and what they do: What explains this variation? We turn to this question in this chapter, by looking first at the structure and activity levels of local parties to understand what they look like and what they do in the contemporary political landscape.

Next, we seek to understand the extent to which local party variation is a reflection of the local and state political environments in which these committees reside. Our data show that local parties are mature organizations that are quite active, and our analyses of structure and activity suggest the environment at both the state and local levels has important effects on organizational form.

Organizational Form at the Local Level: Patterns of Structure and Activity

At the most basic level, local party committees are organizations of individuals; these organizations have institutionalized relationships that help facilitate collective action. As we have discussed, these institutionalized relationships reflect the ways parties are useful to those who associate with, and lend their support to, these party committees. But these institutionalized relationships are also reflective of the environment in which these committees sit. For example, local activists may guide the structure of a local party committee, but this structure may also be constrained by the state party committee, as we discussed in chapter 2. Uncovering these patterns requires an investigation of local parties' organizational form—their organizational structures and the kinds of collective actions in which they engage. Because form represents an adaptation to the environment, it is important to place form within this context and understand its connections to the important features of the environment. Doing so will help us uncover the ways in which party organizations adapt in response to pressures coming from the top down and those coming from the local environment.

To start then, we need to understand the form of local party committees. What, exactly, do we mean by organizational form? The form of any organization ultimately rests on the activities of its members—this is why organizations exist. Organizations have no real existence outside of these activities. Activities remain focused around a goal or set of goals—making money for businesses or winning elections for political parties—and it is the activities that foster the achievement of these goals. Of course, the behavior of individuals can be described as organizational activity only to the extent that it is predictable, regular, and coordinated with others' behavior. We can, from some of these regular patterns of behavior, identify abstract rules, norms, and routines that form the basis of an organization's identity and that might be thought of as characteristic of the organization. For example, most organizations have a designated leader—in the case of local parties, this person is generally the chair of the local party committee. We describe these more regularized patterns of behavior, norms, and rules as structural features, and they are important markers of institutionalization. Included among these features are elements of formal organization (like having a charter and officers), space and staffing patterns, and parts of the organization's external face, such as a telephone listing or website.

In contrast to these structural features, parties also engage in a set of activities that relate directly to their organizational mission and goals. These activities also represent an important element of organizational form, because they express the decisions of organizational members about how they think they can be most effective at their goals in the environments in which they operate. These activities are important, because what parties *do* largely defines what they *are*. Thus, organizational form has two important dimensions: structure and activity.

To measure local party structure and activity in our survey of local party chairs, we utilized the same set of survey items originally used in the Party Transformation Study (PTS) from 1980 (Cotter et al. 1984) and later in the Election Dynamics Project (EDP) in the 1990s by Frendreis and Gitelson (1999). In addition to the common items, there were several new questions, mainly relating to email, website, and social media usage (see appendix for full survey instrument). For all of these questions, respondents were asked to report whether their local party had a particular structural trait or engaged in a specific activity in the 2008 election.

We begin by examining the structural attributes of the 1,187 local party organizations. A summary index of local party structure was based on the presence of 11 structural features: complete set of officers, year-round office, telephone listing, website, email address(es), social media account(s), paid full-time staff, regular annual budget, paid part-time staff, headquarters during campaign season, constitution/charter/formal set of rules.

We divide the sample into Democratic and Republican organizations in figure 3.1 (pg. 52). Several general points can be discerned. First, some basic organizational features are very common. Almost all of these committees have a complete set of officers and some formal set of rules articulated in a constitution or bylaws. As noted previously, the presence of some of these basic features may be driven by state dictates; some state party charters require local organizations to have a constitution or bylaws. But as we also noted, these dictates do not necessarily prevent parties from becoming moribund, so the fact that most organizations here have a complete set of officers is an indication of the continued vitality of local party committees.

Second, while these organizations have some marks of structural maturity, they are not permanent work organizations with an ongoing capacity for collective action. Paid staff of any type are rare; less than 10% of

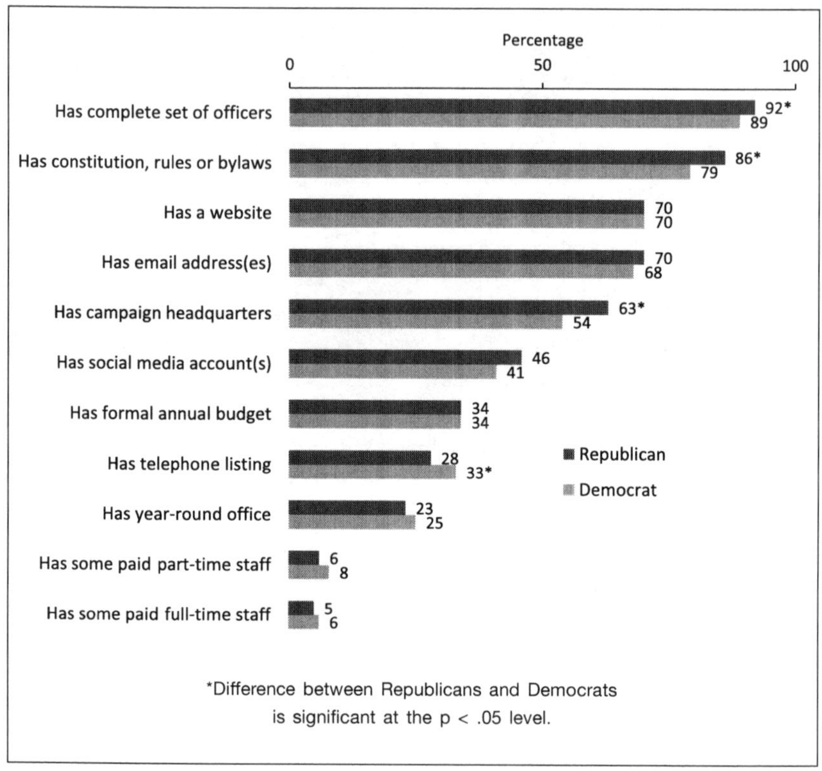

FIGURE 3.1. Structural Characteristics of Local Parties

Democratic and Republican local party committees reported having paid full-time or part-time staff. And while more than half of the organizations had a campaign headquarters, only about a quarter had a year-round office. In this regard, they have not undergone the institutionalization apparent in the national committees or even in most state committees (Holbrook and La Raja 2008). What these data suggest is that a typical local committee has a continuous formal existence, as defined by formal officers and a charter, but an active organizational life that ebbs and flows with the election cycle. This is not altogether surprising, given the external environment. Local party organizations are pressured by state party committees (particularly state party charter requirements) to develop a formal existence, but their primary utility is electoral in nature; the structure of these organizations reflects these environmental influences.

The third point apparent in figure 3.1 is the widespread use of internet tools. About 70% of local committees had a website and email addresses in 2008, and over 40% had social media accounts (e.g., Facebook, Twitter, etc.). Interestingly, these numbers are higher than the number of committees with simple telephone listings. Like most political actors in the 21st century, local party organizations have embraced the place and potential of the internet. This may represent an important change for local party organizations. In the past, most local parties lacked a readily accessible "welcome mat" for local activists who might have an interest in party activity. Few had permanent offices, and most lacked a telephone number. To understand what the local party was all about, an individual had to find out about meeting details, perhaps in the newspaper or by word of mouth, and then actually show up for a meeting. For the shy or marginally committed, this may have been difficult. Today, individuals can "check out" the local party by visiting its website and get a feel for what it stands for, what it does, and how one can get involved. In this way, the web has likely made it easier for people to get involved locally.

How do these data compare to the past? As we have reported previously (Roscoe and Jenkins 2014), local parties have become more mature since 1980.[1] Republican organizations have seen statistically significant jumps in two key indicators—having a complete set of officers and having a formal constitution or bylaws. Democratic organizations have also become more likely to have a formal budget. And both parties are now more likely to have a year-round office or a telephone listing, though the frequency of these traits remains low. There have been declines in none of the structural features since the 1980s. During an era of increasingly candidate-centered campaigning, local parties have become more, not less, institutionalized. This aggregate analysis demonstrates that party organizations are changing and adapting over time, but it does not tell us what features of the environment are driving this adaptation, a question we turn to later in the chapter.

A fourth pattern apparent in figure 3.1 is that the differences between the Democrats and Republicans are minimal. Republicans are more likely, at statistically significant (p < .05) levels, to have campaign headquarters, a complete set of officers, and a constitution, while Democrats are more likely to have a telephone listing. While statistically significant, these differences are not large. Despite the paucity of significant differences between the parties, not all of these local party committees look the same. Simple descriptive analysis reveals considerable variation within the parties in terms of the structure of these local committees. For both the Democrats and Republicans, local party committees reported index scores across the full range of values here (0 to 11). And while the mean was remarkably similar across the parties (5.04 for Democrats and 5.26 for Republicans), there was considerable variation around these means; the standard deviation for Democrats was 2.68 and 2.55 for Republicans. This makes intuitive sense; Republican and Democratic local political parties reside in the same national political environment. This intraparty variation suggests that local parties are adapting to pressures from the state and/or local political environment.

What kinds of activity are undertaken by these local organizations? Our survey of local party chairs measures how many of the following 22 activities the local party engaged in during the 2008 election:

organized door-to-door canvassing	publicized through social media
arranged fundraising events	organized campaign events
assisted a candidate with online fundraising	conducted party fundraising online
	sent mailings to voters
distributed campaign literature	organized telephone campaigns
purchased billboard space	distributed posters or lawn signs
contributed money to candidates	coordinated county-level campaigns
conducted registration drives	conducted get-out-the-vote efforts
utilized public opinion surveys	publicized through press releases
publicized through newspaper advertising	publicized by buying radio/TV time
	publicized through a party website
publicized through email	coordinated local PAC activity

The data presented in figure 3.2 suggest local parties are focused most intently on grassroots activity. Among the 10 most frequent activities, six involve the use of local activists (distributing campaign literature, distributing posters/lawn signs, get-out-the-vote drives, telephone campaigns, canvassing, and registration drives). Importantly, many of these are also labor-intensive activities. Also prominent are activities requiring coordination (organizing campaign and fundraising events).

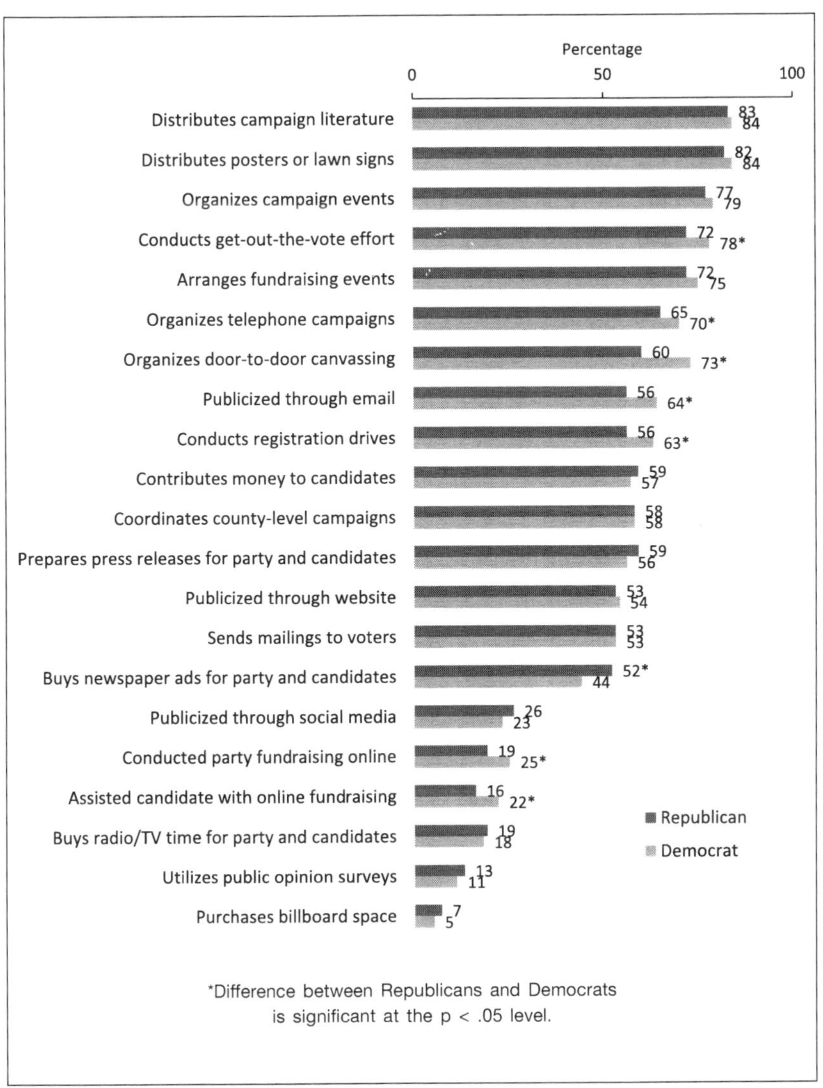

FIGURE 3.2. Activities of Local Parties

Less common are activities that involve the expenditure of money. Just under 60% of local parties contribute money to candidates. Only about half send mailings to voters or purchase newspaper ads, and fewer than 20% buy TV or radio time. Very few engage in polling or purchase billboard space. As we discuss in greater detail in chapter 5, local parties essentially sit on the banks of the major money streams in contemporary elections. Research has demonstrated that in a post-BCRA political landscape, state political parties have shifted away from money-intensive activities and toward labor-intensive activities (Dwyre et al. 2007; La Raja, Orr, and Smith 2006). Our data reveal that local party committees are similarly focusing their work on providing labor not money. This focus on labor-intensive activities across state and local party organizations may serve to heighten the utility of local party organizations as these organizations have the greatest access to committed volunteers. State party committees are often remote to many of the committed activists who wish to volunteer to help the party; they cannot easily show up for a state party event. But they can show up for local party events and the data reveal they are. If the national and state party organizations are focusing on activities that require boots on the ground, local party organizations are in the best position to provide these boots.

In the aggregate, the emphasis on grassroots activity has increased since the 1980s (Roscoe and Jenkins 2014). Parties in 2010 were less likely to buy newspaper ads, buy radio or TV time, or contribute money to candidates. They were more likely to distribute posters or lawn signs, conduct registration drives, organize canvassing, and organize campaign events. Some of the changes have been substantial. For example, the percentage of local organizations conducting canvassing has increased 24% points since 1980 among Democrats, and 12% points among Republicans. Conversely, the percentage purchasing radio or TV time has gone down 15% points among Democrats and 14% points among Republicans. One local party chair in Maine suggested part of the increased emphasis on grassroots activity like canvassing is due to improved lists of voter contacts. She explained that, back "in the seventies and eighties, they would just go to every door because there really wasn't any other way to do it. . . . The addresses were so bad on the voter file that you'd send people out with a walk list and they'd come back in tears because nobody was where they were supposed to be." In her opinion, 2007 marked a turning point in which the walk lists became selective, focused, and accurate enough to make canvassing a highly efficient use of activist resources. This story suggests that the creation of high-quality micro-targeting databases by the national party committees has had important effects on local party activity.

Given the widespread presence of local party websites and email addresses, it is not surprising that these organizations seem to have embraced the use of email and their website to publicize the party and its candidates. Social media lags behind a bit but was still used by about a quarter of local committees. Despite the fact that a majority of committees reported using websites and social media, far more local party committees report having these structures than using them. For instance, 70% of Democratic and Republican local parties reported having a website, but only 54% of Democratic organizations and 53% of Republican organizations reported using them to publicize the party and its candidates. A similar gap emerges for Democratic and Republican social media and Republican email existence and usage, but Democratic Party committees report a much smaller gap for email—68% of them report having an email address, and 64% of them reported publicizing the party and its candidates through email. So while the use of internet tools is fairly widespread, these gaps seem to suggest that effective party use of these forms of activity is emergent. While local parties increasingly have these tools at their fingertips, not all organizations have figured out how to use them.

In contrast, parties have not embraced online fundraising, either for themselves or their candidates. To the extent that parties themselves are learning how to use these tools, it seems unlikely that party assistance will give candidates any advantage beyond what they can do on their own. So in the context of the other activity data, this likely reflects a general orientation away from campaign finance activity for local parties.

Overall, Democratic and Republican local organizations do not differ considerably in the amount and types of activity in which they engage. There is no difference in their overall activity levels: on average, Democratic organizations engage in 11.0 (out of 22) activities and Republicans engage in 10.7, a difference that is not statistically significant. Figure 3.3 (pg. 58) presents histograms of the activity index summing all 22 items, broken down by party. Both distributions are similar, with a peak in the low teens and a secondary spike at zero. As with the structure data, while there are general similarities across the parties, the data reveal considerable variation within the parties; parties report responses across the full range of options (0–22) for the activity index. Once again, these intraparty differences suggest adaptation to forces in the political environment below the national level.

Furthermore, overall activity levels can mask differences across various types of activity, both within and across the parties. For example, figure 3.2 indicates the Democrats have an edge on several grassroots activities (telephone campaigns, canvassing, and registration drives), while the Republicans

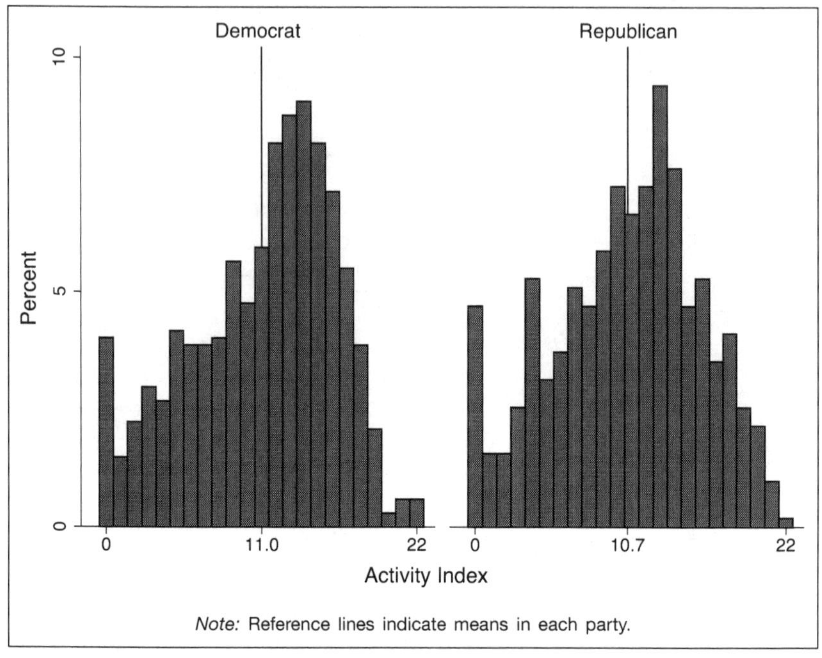

FIGURE 3.3. Histogram of Activity Index by Party

are more likely to buy newspaper ads. To better assess these differences, we have created four sub-indexes that group similar kinds of activities together. These indexes, which range from 0 to 5, are composed of the following items:

Internet Index: conducted party fundraising online; assisted a candidate with online fundraising; publicized through email; publicized through a party website; publicized through social media.

Fundraising Index: arranged fundraising events; conducted party fundraising online; assisted a candidate with online fundraising; contributed money to candidates; coordinated local PAC activity.

Communications Index: publicized through press releases; publicized through newspaper advertising; publicized by buying radio/TV time; sent mailings to voters; purchased billboard space.

> Grassroots Index: organized door-to-door canvassing; distrib-
> uted campaign literature; organized telephone campaigns;
> conducted registration drives; conducted get-out-the-vote
> efforts.

The distributions of these indexes are presented in figure 3.4. First of all, the graphs emphasize the central role of grassroots activities among local parties. Both parties score considerably higher on this index than the others. Second, the data reveal the slightly higher levels of grassroots activity and internet activity among Democrats. The differences in fundraising and communications activities are not statistically significant. Overall the parties are more alike in their activity profiles than different.

As chapter 2 made clear, local parties are located within a state party environment, and this environment may have important effects on what happens at the local level. As we showed, it is common for state organi-

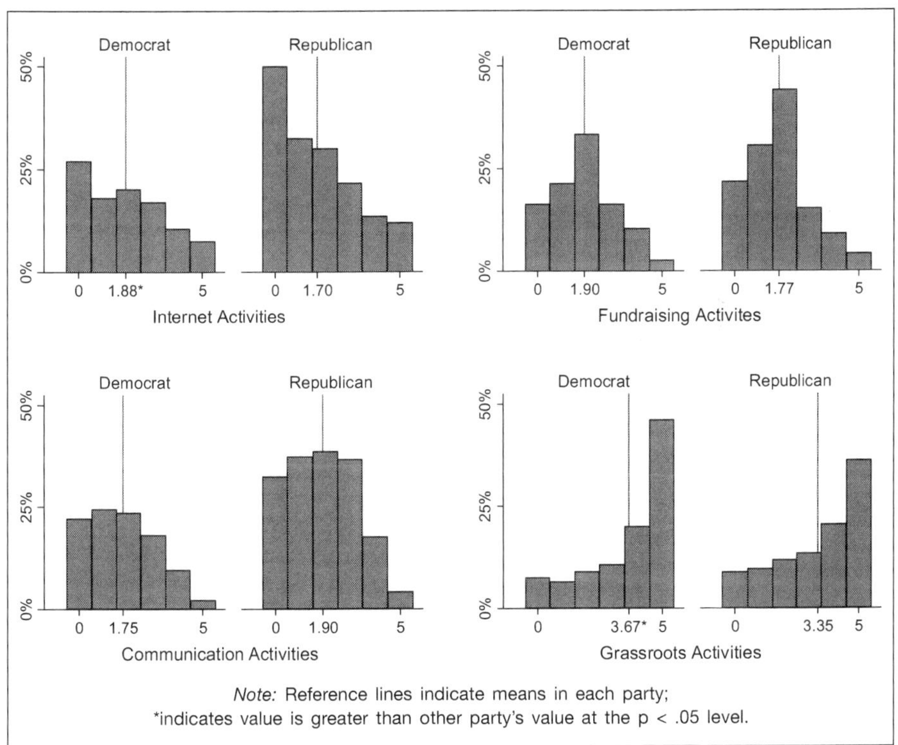

FIGURE 3.4. Histogram of Activity Sub-Indexes by Party

zations to offer assistance to local parties in a number of ways, and this assistance may shape local party structure and activity, a question to which we turn later in the chapter. But in addition to providing assistance to support local party activity, state parties may also engage in activities *with* local party committees. Following from the PTS and the EDP, our survey asked local party committees whether they engaged in any of the following activities jointly with state parties: get-out-the vote (GOTV) drives, shared mailing lists, registration drives, fundraising, and patronage. Overall, these joint activities are less common than most of the local party activities. For instance, the most common joint activity was GOTV drives, as figure 3.5 reveals, with 54% of Democratic and Republican local committees reporting having participated in such activities. Local party committees reported engaging in 12 of the 22 local activities more frequently than this (and two more were about the same).

Nonetheless, these patterns align with the larger picture of local party activity: there is an emphasis on grassroots activity. Over half of local parties undertake joint GOTV efforts with their state party organization. Joint registration drives occur in about a third of the local organizations. Since the 1980s, joint activity has mainly declined or, in some cases, stayed the

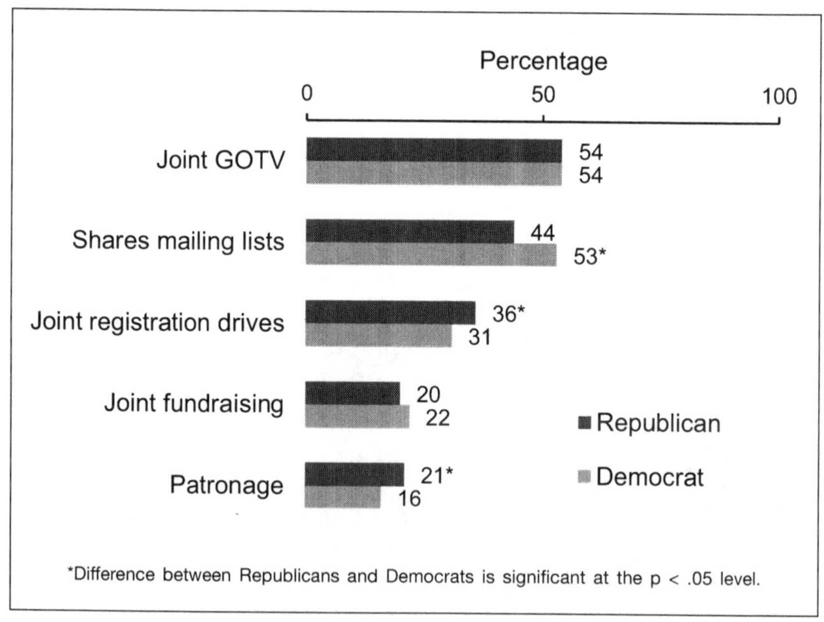

FIGURE 3.5. Joint Activities of State and Local Parties

same (Roscoe and Jenkins 2014). Particularly noteworthy is a paucity of joint fundraising activity, with less than a quarter of all local organizations engaging in this joint activity. Contrasted with the steady levels of cooperation on GOTV efforts, which have emerged as the most common area of mutual assistance, these data support the broader picture of local party activity.

Organizational Form and the Environment

Across the states and across the parties, the structure and activity levels of local party committees vary. Democrats do more door-to-door canvassing; Republicans purchase more newspaper ads. Republicans in Idaho are less active than Republicans in Indiana. Some Democratic committees in Nebraska are active, some are moribund. What drives these varying levels of structural maturity and activity? Why is one committee dormant while another thrives? And how do structure and activity relate? Does structure provide a foundation for high levels of activity? What are the features of the political environment that produce different organizational forms? Understanding the forces that act on organizational form can illuminate the nature of party adaptation.

Like any organization, local party committees reflect their environment. This environment is a complicated one, involving several levels. As we demonstrated in chapter 2, there is ample variation in the state party environment, with some state parties having more effective organizational cultures and providing more assistance to local political parties. Some state parties target their assistance, while others distribute it broadly. To some extent, then, local organizational form may reflect the state political environment in which it resides.[2] But while local party committees may reside in the same state, the local environment in which they reside may be markedly different. Take the Cook County Democrats versus the Knox County Democrats. Both are counties in Illinois, with a decidedly Democratic tilt. However, the former county has 5.2 million residents in a highly urbanized setting, while the latter has 52,000 in a largely rural one. It seems reasonable to assume, given just this one example, that the local environment matters, too. As such, we expect the environmental influences on local party committee form to be multilayered and complex.

To start, the most immediate level is the local one. In the proximate environment, committees are likely to be shaped by political, economic, and social factors. Building from our model of party organization, it might be said that the local environment creates varying degrees of opportunity for people to use local committees toward relevant ends.

Consider first the political environment. The most relevant feature here is the balance of underlying political orientations. A county that leans heavily to one side of the partisan and ideological landscape will present different opportunities for the two committees there, and these will be different in turn from the opportunities in a more evenly balanced county.

In a lopsided district, the out-party may be undeveloped and engage in little activity because there are fewer resources from which to draw. In these communities, there will be fewer activists aligned with the ideology of the out-party, and those activists who do reside there are unlikely to receive any material benefits because the party has little power. Solidary benefits may accrue to activists, but these are also the easiest to satisfy in other settings. For potential candidates, there is also little reason to hitch onto the lost-cause committee and provide its organizational energy. Prudent office seekers are better off distancing themselves from the party and the party label in order to develop a personal following or running as a centrist alternative within the opposing party (as is often done in Massachusetts, for instance). Of course, this does not mean that there is no opportunity here. National elections are always competitive, and even in the bluest of the blue states (e.g., Massachusetts), out-party candidates are often surprisingly competitive in statewide contests. And mounting frustration with the state political context may push some of the party faithful to organize and engage. So there will be some developed and active local party committees in these disadvantaged locations, but they will be few and far between.

For the party advantaged by the local political setting, the situation can be different. Activists are abundant and may realize extensive material, purposive, and solidary benefits. And candidates naturally will hitch themselves to a popular and favored party committee. On the other hand, contributing resources to such a committee may be viewed as inefficient in producing electoral payoffs, given the high probability the party's candidates will win with or without those resources. Furthermore, when the dominant party becomes the vehicle for political advancement, there may be a glut of activists seeking to use the local party organization for their own personal advancement. If there's only one door, everyone may be trying to push through that door at the same time. Strife and struggle may result. Indeed, in one-party-dominant states, the interesting cleavages are often within the dominant party, not between the parties. In these situations, candidates for office often develop their own personal organizations upon which they depend for advancement, not trusting the motives of those in the local party organization. Alternatively, party committees in these situations often seek to remain neutral—not working for or endorsing any candidate when there is a crowded primary field. For instance, Boston mayor Marty Walsh, who was elected after a bruising primary featuring nine candidates and a general election face-off with a fellow Democrat, was endorsed by a few Democratic ward committees in the city but not by the Boston or Suffolk County Democratic Party. As a result, somewhat counterintuitively, we believe that if local parties are shaped by their usefulness, we would expect advantaged parties to lack organizational energy, all else being equal.[3]

In counties that are highly competitive, we are likely to see the most well-developed local committees. Here, much is at stake and all actors with a potential interest in party activity have incentives to support mature and active parties because what they do may matter. To return to our Illinois example mentioned earlier, no matter what the Cook County Democrats or Republicans do, the county will almost surely go Democratic in any electoral contest. But in Lee County, Illinois, where the Democratic state house candidate received just over 48% of the vote in 2008, what the party does may influence the outcome of that election.

Given these hypotheses about the nature of local party competition, we have constructed a local competition variable by taking the party's average vote share in the county/locality in the 2004 and 2008 presidential elections, folded such that it measures how far away this average is, in absolute value terms, from 0% or 100%. Higher scores on this variable suggest more competition, with perfect competition equal to 50; complete lack of competition, an average vote of 0% or 100%, would be coded as 0 for this variable.[4]

It is also likely that the socioeconomic profile of the county population would have some influence on local committees. For the same reasons socioeconomics drive electoral participation (Brady, Verba, and Schlozman 1995), we expect them to shape local party structure and activity. Organizing a political party is costly. Party entrepreneurs and local activists must cover the costs of participating in party maintenance and activity. Communities with larger populations of people with the resources useful for covering these costs should have more mature (and active) parties.

Certainly, a more affluent population simply has more resources available for organizational activity of any type. And those with more education have more of the resources available to cover the civic and knowledge costs of political participation. The well educated, moreover, are also more likely to have well-developed and sophisticated political opinions and will therefore derive greater purposive benefits from party activism. We include two variables to capture these socioeconomic factors: median family income (in $1,000s) and the percentage of the population 25 years or older who have a bachelor's degree or higher (data are taken from the Census Bureau's 2010 American Community Survey, five-year estimates).

Any accounting of local parties must also encompass the unique history of urban areas, which have a history of strong local organizations dating back to the machine era. It is likely that this history has a legacy effect on local committees today. In addition to this legacy effect, it is likely that some of the same features encouraging strong local parties then operate today. The size and scope of urban government provides the opportunities for patronage that feed the desire for material benefits among party activists. Also, population density makes organizing easier. In urban areas, social networks are richer and opportunities for group membership, and the corresponding accumulation of social capital, more available. To measure this factor, we include a variable that codes the percentage of the local population living in urbanized areas (these data come from the 2000 Census).[5]

Even more immediate than the local political and demographic context is the nature of the leadership within the organization itself. As we pointed out in chapter 1, party organizers create the variation in what local organizations do, and entrepreneurs can be important forces in adaptation. Here we consider the effect of one characteristic of the party chair: age. We noted earlier that turnover among chairs is fairly high (Frendreis and Gitelson 1999). Though it is not necessarily the case that younger chairs replace older ones, it does seem likely that younger leadership would be more open to new forms and activities. The average age among the chairs in our study is 56, though it ranges from 22 to 84. We expect younger chairs will oversee more vigorous organizations and should be particularly involved in internet activities.

Beyond the local environment, we also believe the state organizational context will have important effects on local parties. First, the organizational culture of the state party is likely to explain variation in local organizational structure. We believe parties with more effective organizational cultures, as measured by the attribute index, will display greater structural maturity among their local party committees. State party structures with clear goals, innovative approaches, horizontal integration, adept culture management, and so forth, are likely to have vibrant local committees. And as we demonstrated in chapter 2, there is considerable variation on this measure across the states.

Second, state parties often provide direct assistance to local parties, as we showed in chapter 2. Some state parties provided a good deal of assistance, while others provided very little. Furthermore, the standard deviation of this measure also revealed that some state parties were distributing this assistance fairly uniformly, while others were much more targeted in their provision of assistance. It would be surprising if this assistance did not inject life into local organizations. We assess the impact of state assistance by examining the four assistance indexes discussed in chapter 2: core support, special assistance, help with expenses, and internet assistance.

Finally, we need to assess the connections between the two elements of organizational form—structure and activity. Not surprisingly, these two indexes correlate strongly: .61 for the Democrats and .60 for the Republicans. How do the lines of causation run? To be sure, there is likely some reciprocal causality at work. In the long term, an active party may develop structural features as organizers realize the need to support the activities that the party has undertaken. Organizational structure should, in turn, influence the activity levels of local parties. Parties with a more mature structure will have a greater ability to engage in activity, as they will have systems in place that support undertaking these activities. Structural maturity creates capacity for action.

Decisions about structure are likely to be made in the wake of elections, as organizers evaluate the party's performance. As Appleton and Ward (1997) argue, elections are powerful and regular opportunities for reflection and innovation. In other words, the effect of activity on structure is lagged; activity at time *t-1* should influence structure at time *t*. However, with the data here, we can assess only the effect of structure on activity. Our data are cross-sectional, and therefore a lagged model is not possible. Consequently, the structural index is included in the activity models. As structure provides the foundation for activity, we believe this is the most appropriate modeling choice.

Multilevel Model Specification

Given the structure of the data, multilevel modeling, or hierarchical linear modeling, is used to test hypotheses (see Goldstein 2011 and Snijders and Bosker 1999 for general treatments). Multilevel models are appropriate when individual cases (level 1) can be viewed as part of higher-level groups (level 2), and there is an expectation that the relationships of interest may differ across the groups. In standard regression models, the effect of each independent variable on the dependent variable is assumed to be the same for all cases—similarly, the Y-intercept value is also assumed to be constant across all cases. Multilevel models relax one or both of these assumptions. In a sense, multilevel models estimate a separate regression equation for the cases in each level-2 group and allow the parameter estimates from that regression equation to differ for each group. This means the model allows the average value of the dependent variable (more specifically, the Y-intercept) to vary from group to group and may also allow the effect of a dependent variable to differ from one group to another.

There are several virtues to this approach. One is that it avoids a violation of one key assumption of regular regression models—that the errors are uncorrelated. With multilevel data, regression prediction errors may be similar among all cases in a group, and this assumption may not hold. When this assumption is violated, tests of statistical significance may not be accurate. Multilevel models not only account for this error so that estimates are accurate, but they also provide a description of this error variation. The models can tell us how much variation in the intercept or regression coefficients there is across the groups and even whether the intercept and regression coefficients are correlated (for example, whether the effect is stronger in groups where the overall level is lower or higher). These statistics are referred to as random effects, in contrast to fixed effects that describe directly the relationships between the independent and dependent variables.

The data have a clear multilevel structure: each local party committee (level 1) is clustered within a broader state context (level 2). More accurately, there is a three-level grouped structure: local party committees are clustered within state parties, and the state parties are clustered within states. Theoretically, either level, states or state parties, could form the level-2 groups—or a three-level model could be employed. In this case, it was optimal to define a 2-level model with the level-2 groups at the state level or, to put it differently, set aside the group effects at the state party level and focus on the state-level group effects. There is a major, substantive reason for clustering into states at level 2: the state environment creates strong contextual effects for many of the relationships we are examining. At the same time, differences between the parties within the states can be assessed by including a fixed effect variable for party in the models and by interacting each variable with party.

Moreover, this approach is desirable because it avoids defining groups with very few cases. There are many state parties from which only a handful of local committees returned survey responses. Pooling the two state parties increases the average level-2 group size from 14 to 24 and eliminates a couple of singletons (groups with one case). Rules of thumb for level-2 group size in the literature run anywhere from 30/30 (30 groups with 30 cases per group) to 100/10 when there is particular interest in the random effects (variance and covariance components) (Hox 1998). Small level-2 sample sizes are not fatal to a multilevel model, particularly in estimating fixed effects (Clarke and Wheaton 2007), but extensive sparseness can have deleterious effects on the accuracy of estimated parameters. For our models, we have 48 groups with an average group size of 24. Given our interest in both the fixed effects and random effects, this outcome puts the models in the reasonable range for these rules of thumb.

Indeed, the data reveal noteworthy random effects; that is, significant portions of the variance in each dependent variable are distributed across the level-2 groups. The intraclass correlation, which expresses the proportion of the variance attributable to differences among states, for each dependent variable is as follows: structure index = .18, activity index = .09—and for the variables considered in the next chapter—partisan registration = .25, partisan turnout = .19, presidential vote = .13, and House vote = .15. In other words, the levels of our dependent variables vary systematically by state; there is a tendency for all party committees in a state to have similar values. This fact suggests a multilevel model is necessary to properly model the relationships.

In addition to the regular set of independent variables referred to here as fixed effects, multilevel models contain one or more random effects parameters. In this context, *random* means a variable that can take any possible value depending on the outcome of the estimation process, as opposed to fixed effect variables that are measured in advance and take fixed values for each case.

At a minimum, a multilevel model contains a random intercept term. Conceptually, this means the model allows the intercept to vary across the level-2 units (here, states), as opposed to standard regression models where there is a single intercept for all cases in the model. The multilevel model estimates the individual intercept for each state. The intercept reported as the constant in the fixed effects part of the model is the mean of the intercepts across all the states. In the random effects results reported, the "between state variance" is the variance of these intercepts around the overall mean. The "within state variance" represents the residual variance among the individual cases.

For a random intercept model with one predictor, the equation would look as follows:

$$Y_{ij} = b_0 + u_{0j} + \beta X_{ij} + e_{ij}$$

Where Y is the value of the dependent variable for case *i* in state *j*; b_0 is the mean intercept across all states, and u_0 represents the deviation of the intercept in state j from that overall intercept; βX_{ij} is the sum of the products of the coefficient and regressor vectors for the independent variables; and e_{ij} is the residual.

The term u_{0j} is a random effect variable, in that it acts as a variable in the equation, but the values it takes for each case are estimated rather than fixed in advance—note that the value of u_{0j} will be the same for all cases (i) within a state (j). The variance of this term will be referred to as the "between state variance." "Within state variance" is the variance of the residual term, e_{ij}. The substantive importance of allowing the intercepts to vary can be ascertained by considering what proportion of the total variance (between- and within-state) is represented by the variance in the intercept terms (between-state).

To permit the possibility that the effects of each variable might differ between Republican and Democratic party committees, each variable is interacted with party in the models. We report the coefficients for all the variables together, but we also present simple slope coefficients and associated standard errors for Democratic and Republican cases (see Preacher, Curran, and Bauer 2006 for an explanation of simple slopes and corresponding calculations of statistical significance). Because the party variable is coded 0 for Democrats and 1 for Republicans, the main coefficient for each variable gives the slope for Democrats, and the interaction term indicates how the slope for Republicans differs from Democrats. The simple slope for Democrats is the same as the main coefficient, and the simple slope for Republicans is simply the sum of this coefficient and the interaction term. More importantly, the simple slope calculation for Republicans also produces a recalculated standard error, which allows for an assessment of whether this slope differs from zero (whereas the interaction term assesses whether the Republican slope differs from the Democratic slope). In this way, the simple slopes permit hypotheses testing of each variable separately and directly for both Democratic and Republican cases.

Multilevel models also permit a random effect for the slope of any independent variable in the model. In other words, rather than fitting all the individual cases to a single regression line, the model permits the slope (as well as the intercept) to vary state-to-state. Again, the reported regression coefficient in the fixed effects portion of the model is the overall slope for all cases. The slope variance gives the variance of the slopes among the states around this overall slope. Random slope specifications will be employed in the next chapter, in the models examining the effect of activity on electoral outcomes.

Modeling Local Party Structure

Table 3.1 (pg. 70) displays the results of the models examining the influences on local committee structure. First, the models support the importance of the local environment. We find that local committees are more mature among populations that are more urbanized and better educated, as expected, and the effects are similar for Republicans and Democrats. Income, however, is not a significant predictor. When it comes to party organizations, civic resources, not monetary ones, seem to be the key factor.

Local organizations are also more mature in more competitive areas, though the effect is not particularly large and is statistically significant only for Republicans. Among these Republican committees, a 5% point difference in the competition variable (which ranges from 0 to 50 and has a standard deviation of 8.7%) is associated with a change of only 0.17 on the structural index (which ranges from 0 to 11). Competitive Republican parties are more mature, but not much; the difference between a Republican party in a county where it completely dominates (or is completely dominated) and a perfectly competitive district is only about 2 more structural attributes (1.7 to be exact), hardly an overwhelming difference. Finally, there is support for the hypothesis that younger chairs lead more structurally mature committees, but only among the Democrats, and the effect size is small. The model suggests a 20-year-old chair would have a local party committee with one more structural attribute than a 60-year-old chair.

Considering the state-level environment, it is clear that cultural effectiveness boosts local Democratic party structure. A one-unit change in the cultural effectiveness index is associated with a 1.246 change in the 11-point structure index. A one standard deviation change in cultural effectiveness, 0.34, is associated with a change of 0.42 in the structure index. Though not overly large, it is a stronger effect than that of local party competition. However, the simple slopes reveal an important interaction effect: the effectiveness of the state party organizational culture has an impact only on local party structure among Democratic parties. The simple slope for Republican committees is 0.162, which falls outside the region of statistical significance.

Finally, we find evidence that some, but only some, of the state assistance variables support local structure. Internet assistance is statistically significant for both parties. Because internet features (having a website and email addresses) are part of the structure index, this is not surprising. Also, this may be an area where the technical knowledge is not available at the local level, and so state assistance can make a big difference. Special

Table 3.1. The Influences on Local Party Structure

Fixed Effects	Coef.	SE	Simple Slope Dem.	SE	Simple Slope Rep.	SE
Constant	−1.322					
Party	2.353	2.976				
Urban %	.028***	.003				
X Party	−.009	.005	.028***	.003	.019***	.004
Median Income $1,000s	−.001	.006				
X Party	.010	.009	−.001	.006	.009	.008
% Bachelor's Degree	.053***	.011				
X Party	.001	.018	.053***	.011	.053***	.015
Competition	.021	.011				
X Party	.013	.017	.021	.011	.034*	.014
Chair Age	−.025**	.007				
X Party	.021	.011	−.025**	.007	−.004	.008
Cultural Effectiveness	1.246*	.554				
X Party	−1.084	.765	1.246*	.554	.162	.543
Core Assist	.332	.202				
X Party	−.003	.321	.332	.202	.329	.251
Special Assist	.626***	.127				
X Party	−.350	.212	.626***	.127	.276	.172
Expenses Assist	−.147	.172				
X Party	.723**	.263	−.147	.172	.577**	.201
Internet Assist	.424**	.159				
X Party	.010	.223	.424**	.159	.434**	.157
Random Effects						
Between State Variance	1.044					
Within State Variance	3.657					
Observations	898					
Groups	47					

Note: Fixed effects entries are unstandardized regression coefficients; SE is standard error; *p <.05; **P < .01; ***P < .001.

assistance boosts local structure for the Democrats but not the Republicans. In contrast, help with expenses fosters Republican organizations but not Democratic ones. Interestingly, core assistance—help with office space and staff—has a positive effect on structure for both parties, but the coefficients fail to reach statistical significance.

Modeling Local Party Activity

The preceding analysis found evidence that both the statewide environment and the local context shape the structural characteristics of local parties. Adaptation is being driven from the top down and the bottom up. But what about activity? Is local party activity similarly influenced by variables at the local and state level? How do these influences differ from those shaping structure? And, what role does structure play in setting the stage for activity?

To answer these questions, we modeled activity as a function of the same variables used to predict structure. In addition, we include the structural index variable here as a predictor of activity. As discussed earlier, we see structure as a more durable dimension of organizational form and one that provides the capacity for local organizations to engage in activity around election time. In this conceptualization, contextual forces can have both direct effects on activity as well as indirect effects through their influence on structure. Our causal model, therefore, looks like this:

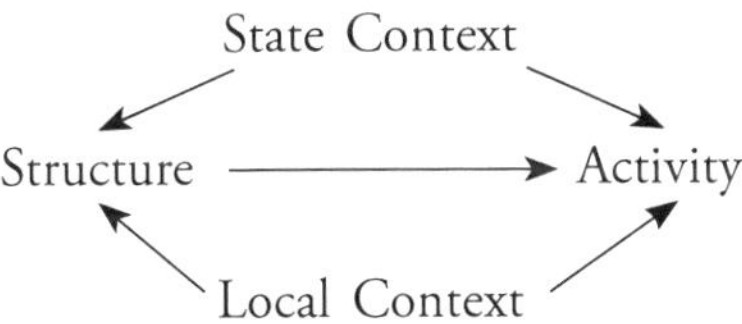

In addition to modeling the influences on overall activity, we also break out activity into its various components by using the four sub-indexes for grassroots activity, communication activity, fundraising activity, and internet activity. The full model results are presented in table 3.2 (pg. 72), and the simple slopes, with appropriate standard errors, are presented separately in table 3.3 (pg. 73).

Consider first the local environmental variables, which are grouped together toward the top of each table. The first striking finding is the powerful effect structure has on activity. The structural index variable is significant in each model for both parties. The effect sizes are notable. Recall

Table 3.2. The Influences on Local Party Activity

Fixed Effects	All Coef.	SE	Grass. Coef.	SE	Comm. Coef.	SE	Funds. Coef.	SE	Web Coef.	SE
Constant	6.058		1.485		2.637		.935		.901	
Party	−2.836	4.603	.222	1.714	−2.075	1.626	−1.581	1.406	−1.041	1.406
Structure	1.078***	.071	.267***	.026	.178***	.024	.185***	.022	.359***	.022
X Party	.035	.112	.031	.041	.016	.038	.011	.035	−.009	.036
Urban %	−.001	.006	.001	.002	−.003	.001	.0002	.002	.0004	.002
X Party	.001	.009	.004	.003	−.002	.003	−.003	.003	.001	.002
Median Income	.005	.011	−.001	.004	−.001	.004	.003	.003	.002	.003
X Party	.017	.016	.006	.006	.005	.005	.007	.005	.008	.005
% Bachelor's Degree	.007	.019	−.002	.007	−.003	.006	.012*	.006	.016**	.006
X Party	−.006	.031	−.006	.011	.003	.011	−.003	.010	−.007	.010
Competition	.065**	.019	.021**	.007	.021**	.006	.010	.006	.005	.006
X Party	−.059*	.029	−.031**	.010	−.018	.010	−.008	.009	−.002	.009
Chair Age	−.004	.013	.001	.005	.001	.004	−.001	.004	−.012**	.004
X Party	.027	.019	.012	.007	.005	.006	.010	.006	.006	.006
Cultural Effectiveness	−.766	.824	.032	.310	−.663*	.295	−.206	.250	−.247	.246
X Party	.639	1.165	−.161	.436	.637	.414	.305	.355	.114	.351
Core Assist 4	.643	.341	.004	.124	.023	.117	.495***	.106	.259*	.111
X Party	−.029	.547	.189	.199	.018	.187	−.226	.170	−.173	.179
Special Assist 1	1.100***	.222	.249**	.081	.266***	.076	.206**	.069	.272***	.073
X Party	−.132	.365	.002	.133	.083	.125	−.142	.113	−.070	.120
Expenses Assist 3	.159	.290	.011	.106	.146	.099	−.076	.090	.059	.094
X Party	.344	.450	−.032	.164	−.053	.154	.250	.139	.238	.147
Internet Assist 2	.848**	.273	.272**	.099	.274**	.093	.130	.084	.048	.089
X Party	−.783*	.383	−.261*	.139	−.196	.131	−.134	.119	−.012	.125
Random Effects										
Between State Var.	.674		.130		.135		.050		.013	
Within State Var.	10.908		1.433		1.258		1.054		1.205	
Observations	898		898		898		898		898	
Groups	47		47		47		47		47	

Note: Fixed effects entries are unstandardized regression coefficients; Grass. = Grassroots Activity, Comm. = Communications Activity, Funds. = Fundraising Activity, Web = Internet Activity; SE is standard error; *p<.05; **P<.01; ***P<.001.

Table 3.3. Simple Slopes for the Interaction Variables in Table 3.2

	All		Grass.		Comm.		Funds.		Web	
Fixed Effects	Dem	Rep	Dem	Rep	Dem	Rep	Dem	Rep	Dem	Rep
Structure	1.078***	1.114***	.267***	.298***	.178***	.194***	.185***	.196***	.359***	.349***
	(.071)	(.089)	(.026)	(.032)	(.024)	(.030)	(.022)	(.027)	(.022)	(.029)
Urban %	−.001	−.001	.001	.005	−.003	−.005*	.0002	−.003	.0004	.002
	(.006)	(.007)	(.002)	(.002)	(.001)	(.002)	(.002)	(.002)	(.002)	(.002)
Median Income	.005	.022	−.001	.005	−.001	.005	.003	.010*	.002	.011*
	(.011)	(.013)	(.004)	(.005)	(.004)	(.004)	(.003)	(.004)	(.003)	(.004)
% Bachelor's Degree	.007	.002	−.002	−.008	−.003	−.0004	.012*	.009	.016**	.009
	(.019)	(.026)	(.007)	(.009)	(.006)	(.009)	(.006)	(.008)	(.006)	(.008)
Competition	.065**	.006	.021**	−.009	.021**	.004	.010	.001	.005	.003
	(.019)	(.023)	(.007)	(.009)	(.006)	(.008)	(.006)	(.007)	(.006)	(.007)
Chair Age	−.004	.023	.001	.013*	.001	.006	−.001	.009*	−.012**	−.005
	(.013)	(.014)	(.005)	(.005)	(.004)	(.005)	(.004)	(.004)	(.004)	(.004)
Cultural Effectiveness	−.766	−.127	.032	−.128	−.663*	−.025	−.206	.099	−.247	−.133
	(.824)	(.830)	(.310)	(.310)	(.295)	(.295)	(.250)	(.253)	(.246)	(.251)
Core Assist 4	.643	.614	.004	.193	.023	.041	.495***	.269*	.259*	.086
	(.341)	(.430)	(.124)	(.156)	(.117)	(.147)	(.106)	(.133)	(.111)	(.141)
Special Assist 1	1.100***	.968**	.249**	.251*	.266***	.349**	.206**	.064	.272***	.202*
	(.222)	(.294)	(.081)	(.107)	(.076)	(.100)	(.069)	(.091)	(.073)	(.096)
Expenses Assist 3	.159	.503	.011	−.021	.146	.093	−.076	.174	.059	.296**
	(.290)	(.345)	(.106)	(.126)	(.099)	(.118)	(.090)	(.107)	(.094)	(.113)
Internet Assist 2	.848**	.064	.272**	.011	.274**	.078	.130	−.003	.048	.035
	(.290)	(.271)	(.099)	(.099)	(.093)	(.093)	(.084)	(.084)	(.089)	(.088)

Note: Simple slopes are calculated on the basis of the results in Table 3.2; Grass. = Grassroots Activity, Comm. = Communications Activity, Funds. = Fundraising Activity, Web = Internet Activity; standard errors are in parentheses; *p<.05; **P<.01; ***P<.001.

that the structural index ranges from 0 to 11 (with a standard deviation of 2.6) and the activity index ranges from 0 to 22 (with a standard deviation of 5.2). In the first model examining overall activity, there is about a 1:1 effect—each additional structural indicator is associated with one additional activity. Looked at another way, a one standard deviation change in structure is associated with half a standard deviation change in overall activity levels. The sub-indexes range from 0 to 5 (with standard deviations between 1.3 and 1.7), so the coefficients are appropriately smaller, but the effects are nearly as strong. Structure has the biggest effects on web activity, followed closely by grassroots activity. For each additional standard deviation increase in structure, web activity goes up just over half a standard deviation and grassroots activity goes up just under half a standard deviation. The effect is a bit smaller for communication and fundraising, though still quite strong. Overall, the results support the supposition that more structurally mature parties have the capacity to engage in higher levels of activity.

In contrast, the results suggest demographics have very little connection to activity levels. None of them predicts overall activity levels. The results differ sharply from the structure model, where urbanization and affluence were strong predictors. These patterns suggest the characteristics of the local population mainly have an indirect effect on activity. Urbanized and affluent communities have more structurally mature parties, and this maturity fosters activity. In some areas, however, demographics shape activity above and beyond this indirect effect. There are a few significant relationships among the sub-indexes: in more highly educated communities, Democratic parties engage in more fundraising activities and Republican parties are more active on the web; similarly, more affluent areas see more Republican activity in fundraising and on the internet. In contrast, Republicans are less involved in communication activities in urbanized areas.

We had observed that the level of interparty competition had minimal effects on structure, and they were limited to Republicans. Here, we find similarly small effects, but they are limited to Democrats. Competition has a statistically significant impact on overall activity, as well as grassroots and communications activities, but only among Democrats. The effects are surprisingly weak. A difference of 5% points in the competition variable is associated with a difference of only .325 in the overall activity index for Democrats. Consider two Democratic party committees, one in a county where they regularly win (or lose) by 25% points and one where they garner only 50% of the vote on average. The results here suggest the latter would engage in only 1.6 more activities (out of 22). The effects are similarly small for grassroots and communications activity. So competition builds structural maturity for Republicans but increased activity for Democrats, although the effect sizes are small in both cases. Why structural maturity and activity levels are so unconnected to competition is an interesting puzzle, which we explore more in chapter 5.

We hypothesized younger chairs would lead more active organizations, but we find this to be true only for Democrats and internet activity. Younger Democrats lead organizations that are more active on the web. This might have been expected, given the inverse relationship between age and digital nativism. What was not expected is the positive relationship, among Republicans, between the age of the chair and the level of grassroots and fundraising activity. The magnitude of all these relationships are not large, however. It may be tempting to conclude that chairs, as part of the local context, have little impact on their party organizations, but this moves well beyond our data. Age is only one characteristic of chairs that might matter. Interestingly, we examined ideological extremity, under the expectation that more extreme chairs would be more active. However, this hypothesis failed even at the bivariate level: ideological extremity is not correlated, at statistically significant levels, with structure or activity (neither overall nor the sub-indexes). It's also possible that younger chairs are more innovative—and it may even be the case that youth operates differently in different party cultures. One Georgia Democratic chair suggested the Republicans tend to be more paternal, while the Democrats are often energized by young activists. Unfortunately, our survey did not ask any other questions about chair characteristics that might be applied here. Indeed, capturing the relevant kinds of characteristics—dynamic leadership abilities, intelligence, openness to innovation, interpersonal skills—might be difficult to measure in a survey.

What about state-level factors? Do features of the state party context shape local activity? We find, first, that cultural effectiveness is not important here. Only one coefficient is significant, and the sign is in the wrong direction: Democratic parties are more active in communications in less effective parties. Recall that organizational culture had very strong effects on structural maturity for the Democrats. The findings, taken together, suggest culture may work only indirectly to influence activity. State organizational culture shapes local party structure, and structure shapes activity. This finding may reflect the nature of these variables. Organizational culture is likely a relatively stable environmental characteristic, so it may be natural that it most strongly influences structure, the more stable dimension of local form. Furthermore, measures of organizational culture ask about rules, norms, and behavior patterns; as we argued earlier in this chapter, these rules, norms, and behavior patterns relate more to the identity and maintenance of the organization than to its objectives. To be sure, the ultimate goal of any organization is the achievement of its goals, but culture is focused on building the foundation of an effective organization.

The other major way state parties can shape local activity is through direct assistance. Our data show that core assistance—help with office space and staffing—has effects that are limited to fundraising and, for Democrats, web activity. Beyond these areas, core assistance does not encourage activity—nor does it build organizational structure. One reason for these non-findings may be found in the relative rarity of this kind of assistance. Only about 4% of local parties get help with office space, and 9% receive staff assistance. State parties are simply not in the business of propping up local parties in these ways. Their reasons in the small number of cases where they do may be idiosyncratic and unrelated to the needs or outputs of local parties.

In contrast, special assistance plays a consistently strong role. It is statistically significant in every model for both parties, with just one exception (Republicans and fundraising). Why is this kind of aid so important in shaping what local parties do? One possible answer is the role of expertise. The kinds of activities that load strongly on this factor require special knowledge, training, or expertise: assistance with financial record keeping, legal advice, campaign training. Local party organizers and activists may lack the ability to do these kinds of things. State parties, on the other hand, can hire this expertise and share it across the local organizations in ways that are efficient and realize economies of scale. Furthermore, as we argued in chapter 2, special assistance does not require a long-term commitment on the part of the state party. This special assistance can be provided in the months leading up to an election in order to foster activity designed to win the election. It is not surprising that this targeted assistance produces results.

Assistance with campaign or operating expenses does not have the same kind of impact. Though they do make Republicans more active in web activities, overall they do not have a discernable effect. As was suggested for core assistance, this may again reflect the fact that state parties are not providing this assistance in almost all cases. There is just not that much variation to create patterns of covariation. It may also reflect the fact that the specialized niche of local party organizations is labor, not money. As we show in chapter 5, the money flows largely go on above the heads of local party committees, so there is little money coming in with little effect.

Finally, we find some limited effects for internet assistance. Surprisingly, one area this assistance does not affect is internet activity. Instead, this kind of help with website development and social media corresponds with more grassroots activity, more communication activity, and higher levels of activity overall, but only for Democrats. Again, this may reflect the Democratic 50-state strategy and the Obama campaign's focus on developing sophisticated internet fundraising and targeting operations.

Conclusion: State and Local Environments

We began this book with the theory that local party committees are adaptive organizations that respond to changes in the political environment. This political environment contains state-level factors, as state party organizations often engage in actions to shape local party committees. This can result from managing the culture of the party organization in order to increase effectiveness and from providing assistance to local parties to jump-start their organization and activities. While chapter 2 demonstrated the potential for this type of influence, the analysis here confirmed this influence. The assistance that state party organizations provide to local party committees has strong effects in shaping both the structure and the activity levels of local parties—states that provide more assistance induce greater party development and activity, even when controlling for other features of the political environment.

However, the influence of cultural effectiveness is mainly limited to influences on the structure of local party committees and really only for the Democrats. Organizational culture scholars have often pointed to the difficulty in managing organizational culture, and this analysis seems to confirm their findings in the realm of political organization. Of course, one might argue that political parties probably are not really focusing on managing organizational culture, to the extent that they know about the concept at all. If national and state parties were to focus more efforts on this, perhaps they would be more successful. That may be true; all we can say at this point in time is that the organizational culture of a state party organization has only limited influence on local party committees. Despite these limited findings for organizational culture, the analysis shows top-down management of political parties is possible. Assistance from state party organizations shapes structure and activity in both Democratic and Republican organizations, so smart state parties should focus on this. One way to get results from local parties is to seed them with targeted special assistance.

Of course, there are also limits to the effectiveness of adaptation forced from the top down as local party committees are strongly shaped by the local environment in which they reside. Education and population density in particular play roles in shaping the structure of local party organizations, and this structure in turn shapes the activity of local parties. Furthermore, the level of competition in a district also shapes local party activity, with more competition inducing more activity, as expected.

Thus, the form of local party committees is shaped by the environment in which they reside. But, of course, that leaves us with the so-what question. If local parties are geared towards electoral activity, then how local parties look and how they operate does not really matter unless this activity has some impact on election outcomes. Absent any effect, then all this activity is really superfluous. So now, we turn to our final question about local party committees—does their activity matter?—in the next chapter.

CHAPTER 4

The Electoral Payoff

In various ways, local party structure and activity reflect the environment—both the local context and the broader statewide setting. The form of local parties is responsive to both state efforts to manage that form and to the local political and socioeconomic environment. As hypothesized, local parties are adaptive organizations. Fundamental to our investigations of local political parties is the assumption that local parties matter. Though an electoral payoff is not the only reason political actors might channel resources to local party committees and encourage activity, it is the primary rationale. And as the prior chapter showed, activity is higher in contexts where expectations of electoral benefit are heightened.

But, are these assumptions reasonable? Does the activity of local parties really create an electoral payoff? There is very little prior research on this question. The key study by Frendreis, Gibson, and Vertz (1990) examined this question using data from the 1980–1984 Party Transformation Study. Their results showed small effects for local party activity levels on US House and gubernatorial election outcomes and no effects on state legislative, US Senate, or presidential election outcomes. Moreover, the significant effects are not consistent and the effect sizes are quite small. Among the 11 models they test across the three time periods (1980, 1982, and 1984) and the various races, only three activity variables are statistically significant, and these were all for Democratic party activity. They do find, however, that local party activity has a more meaningful impact on the probability that a party candidate will emerge at all in House and state legislative races.

These results seem discouraging, but there is reason to expect a bigger impact than they found. First, they include measures of local party *structure* in their models alongside the activity variables. As chapter 3 demonstrated, structure is best understood as a foundation for activity rather than a competing influence. After all, having a formal charter doesn't gain a candidate votes in the same way canvassing might. Structure builds the capacity for activity and, indeed, is highly predictive of activity, but it is activity that has an impact on voters and elections. The inclusion of these structure variables introduces some collinearity in the model, and this may have reduced the observable effect sizes for the activity variables.

Second, it makes sense to broaden the search beyond candidate vote shares to consider potential mobilization effects. After all, parties historically have been central to the process of identifying and turning out voters. This role may have diminished for some period of time (Rosenstone and Hansen 1993), but it has increased since the time of the Frendreis, Gibson, and Vertz study, as chapter 3 showed. The development of 50-state strategies by the two major parties represents a return to focusing on the ground game. Registration and turnout operations are labor intensive, and local parties have the ability to attract and activate a loyal group of local partisans, ready to help out with phone calls, canvassing, or registration drives. And as chapter 2 showed, this is exactly the sort of assistance state parties are most commonly providing to local party committees; rather than providing money or operating expenses, state parties seem to be focusing on providing the sorts of assistance that foster local party activities in these areas. Candidates can get money for advertising anywhere, but parties remain a good option for foot soldiers. For these reasons, we might expect party activity to correlate with partisan registration rates and partisan turnout rates.

Analyzing the Effects of Party Activity

To test for signs of an electoral payoff for local party activity, we will start by considering the overall level of activity, as measured by the 22-point activity index scale utilized in chapter 3. Later we will look at the individual activities and their relationships with the electoral variables.

We will look at the effect of activity on two mobilization variables and two vote outcome variables. Our first mobilization variable is partisan registration, which we measure at the county level. Not all states require party registration, and so it is available in only 27 of the states in our dataset; as a result, the number of cases in the analyses of partisan registration is 591. This variable codes the percentage of registered voters in the locality (county or town) who are registered under the local party's label.

Measuring turnout is a bit more complicated. We expect more party activity will lead to higher levels of turnout, but we really expect this effect to be a *partisan* one. Local Republican parties, for example, will attempt to mobilize Republicans and vice versa for Democratic parties. Turnout numbers at the county level, reflected in ballots cast, do not provide a way to separate Democratic from Republican voters. Thus, in order to assess partisan turnout rates, we have divided the number of votes cast in the county for the party's presidential candidate by the voting age population in the county.

Our vote outcome variables include the local (county/town/district) vote share for the party's own presidential candidate and its own US House candidate. We are not able to examine state legislative races, because almost no states report these data at the county level.

The county-level presidential data are from *Congressional Quarterly* and were accessed through the Census Bureau's data interface. County-level House returns and party registration figures come from data provided by Dave Leip.[1] Both of these sources are supplemented by data on Massachusetts towns from the *Boston Globe* website and from official state websites for Alaska, Connecticut, North Dakota, Rhode Island, and Virginia.

Because preliminary diagnostics indicated significant model improvement, the multilevel models are specified with a random slope term for the activity index variable as well as a random intercept term. This specification allows the slope for the activity index to vary by state, with the fixed effect slope expressing the mean slope across all states. Using the notation introduced in chapter 3, the equation is as follows:

$$Y_{ij} = b_0 + u_{0j} + b_1 X_{ij} + u_{1j} + \beta X_{ij} + e_{ij}$$

Where Y is the value of the dependent variable for case *i* in state *j*; b_0 is the overall mean of the intercepts, and u_0 represents the deviation of the intercept in state *j* from that overall mean; $b_1 X_{ij}$ is the fixed effect slope term for the activity variable, and u_1 represents the deviation of the slope in state *j* from that overall slope; βX_{ij} is the sum of the products of the coefficient and regressor vectors for the other independent variables; and e_{ij} is the residual.

Table 4.1 (pg. 82) presents the results of the multilevel models. First, it is worth examining the control variables in the model. Here, as in chapter 3, we include the urbanization rate, the percentage of residents with a college degree, and the median income in $1,000s. However, we expect these variables to have opposite effects for Democratic and Republican candidates. In the partisan registration model, the data reveal higher registration rates for Democrats when the county has higher urbanization and lower

Table 4.1. The Influence of Local Party Electoral Activity on Election Outcomes

Fixed Effects	Own Party Registration	Own Party Turnout	Presidential Vote	House Vote
Constant	40.837	16.182	30.100	39.884
Party	−16.668***	17.416***	37.245***	13.116**
	(3.440)	(1.720)	(2.479)	(4.010)
Urban %	.052*	−.011	.071***	.059*
	(.023)	(.012)	(.016)	(.027)
X Party	−.106**	−.108***	−.173***	−.160***
	(.034)	(.018)	(.026)	(.042)
Median Income $1,000s	−.178***	−.018	−.138***	−.153**
	(.040)	(.024)	(.033)	(.055)
X Party	.266***	.155***	.177***	.333***
	(.058)	(.035)	(.050)	(.083)
% Bachelor's Degree	.098	.410***	.486***	.350***
	(.077)	(.042)	(.058)	(.098)
X Party	.043	−.500***	−.868***	−.548***
	(.126)	(.067)	(.095)	(.157)
Activity	.136	.265**	.621***	.521**
	(.184)	(.083)	(.125)	(.168)
X Party	.096	−.287**	−.688***	−.719**
	(.219)	(.105)	(.152)	(.239)
Random Effects				
Between State Variance	126.346	24.216	61.908	95.515
Within State Variance	124.045	65.067	138.910	366.617
Activity Slope Variance	.278	.067	.204	.068
Activity-Intercept Covariance	−4.545	−.985	−3.550	−2.167
Observations	591	1182	1182	1181
Groups	27	48	48	48
Simple Slopes				
Activity for Democrats	.136	.265**	.621***	.521**
	(.184)	(.083)	(.125)	(.168)
Activity for Republicans	.232	−.022	−.067	−.199
	(.197)	(.088)	(.132)	(.183)

Note: Fixed effects entries are unstandardized regression coefficients; standard errors are in parentheses; *p<.05; **P<.01; ***P<.001.

median income. Republicans have higher partisan registration rates in coun-ties that are less urbanized and more affluent. The education variable is not significant.

In the partisan turnout models, the expectations of differential effects by party are not as strong. As Brady, Verba, and Schlozman (1995) point out, socioeconomic resources raise the probability of turnout across the board. At the same time, our variable captures *who* voters chose, as well as whether they showed up, so a partisan effect is likely. Urbanization has no effect on Democratic turnout, but it is associated with lower turnout for the Republicans. Similarly, income is not associated with Democratic turnout, but Republican turnout is higher in more affluent counties. Education has interesting effects. It is strongly associated with higher levels of turnout for Democrats, but the effect on Republican turnout is slightly negative.

Overall, the control variables are generally significant and some of the effect sizes are notably large—this conclusion holds, as well, for the other models in this chapter, as we will see. This provides some assurance that we are isolating the effect of local party activity.

The effect of activity is generally stronger for turnout than registra-tion. In the partisan registration models, the activity index is positive but not quite statistically significant. Moreover, the effect appears not to differ between the parties. The interaction term is not significant, and the simple slope calculations reveal a slope of .136 for the Democrats and .232 for the Republicans; neither is significant.[2] The effect sizes are not insubstantial—a difference of five activities would be associated with a difference of around 1% point increase in the registration rate. However, the standard errors are large and we therefore cannot reject the null hypotheses here. In the partisan turnout models, the effect is significant, but only for Democrats. An increase of about four activities is associated with an increased vote share of 1% point.

These results are somewhat surprising, as we expected activity levels to have an impact on both registration and turnout levels. These findings may reflect the fact that local parties are more likely to engage in activities that are focused on voter turnout than voter registration. For instance, 78% of Democratic parties and 72% of Republican parties conducted get-out-the-vote drives in 2008. More than 60% of both parties also conducted telephone and door-to-door campaigns, efforts which most likely focused on voter turnout. All of these efforts, as well as other efforts that are more focused on outcomes such as distributing campaign literature and poster and lawn signs, occur more frequently than registration activities. But local party activities focused on registration are not uncommon either; 63% of

Democratic organizations and 56% of Republican organizations conducted registration drives. It may simply be that many party activities are focused on getting people to vote, while only one of these activities is actually focused on increasing registration levels. The nonfindings may also reflect the importance of other factors that shape registration rates. As Norrander and Wendland (2014) note, voter registration is influenced by state primary rules, even among states with party registration requirements.

The strong, positive effect for Democrats makes sense. Personal contact, particularly personal canvassing, has been shown to increase turnout levels (Gerber and Green 2000). The lack of impact for Republicans is a puzzle, though—a puzzle we return to later in this chapter. Interestingly, this pattern repeats itself in the models for presidential and House vote. The data suggest Democratic activity has strong effects on Democratic candidate vote share (measured here as percentages of the total votes cast). Each additional activity used by the local Democratic Party increased Obama's vote share in the county by .621% points and the Democratic House candidate's share by .521% points. Considering that the 22-point activity index has a standard deviation of around 5, these coefficients suggest fairly substantial effects. Moving a standard deviation up on the activity index would appear to boost the presidential vote about 3% points and the House vote about 2.5% points. Most candidates would be thrilled with such assistance.

But the Republican candidates appear to get no such help. The simple slopes for Republicans are actually negative but not statistically significant. In general, then, our findings at first glance resemble those of Frendreis, Gibson, and Vertz (1990) in that the positive effects of activity seem limited to Democrats.

However, it is also possible that contextual factors are obscuring the effects of Republican activity. In this regard, it is interesting to note the large and negative covariances between the activity and intercept random effects. Because the model includes a random effect for the activity index variable (i.e., the slope of this variable is allowed to vary across states) and a random effect for the intercept (i.e., the intercept of the equation is allowed to vary across states), it is possible to assess whether these two random parameters are related. The activity-intercept covariance measures this relationship, and the results suggest activity has a much larger slope when the intercept is lower. In other words, local party activity matters much more when the party, on average across the state, does worse. Local activity has the weakest impact in states where the party dominated elections. When the covariances are converted into correlations, the magnitude of the relationships is arresting. The correlation in both the partisan registration and partisan turnout models is –.77. For the presidential vote model that includes the interaction term, the correlation is –.99. In the House vote model, the correlation is –.85. These correlations suggest that the competitive context of the state mediates the relationship between activity and electoral outcomes.

Why might the competitive context moderate the effects of activity on election outcomes? Past research has suggested the effects of activity on election outcomes are complicated and contingent on context. Frendreis, Gibson, and Vertz raise this possibility: "In some cases, the strongest electoral payoffs for local party activity may come under fairly limited conditions" (1990, 229). Though they do not model these interaction effects, we expect that the actors within state parties think differently and allocate resources differently depending on the competitive context. When the party is in a competitive environment or when the party is disfavored by the statewide partisan context, we expect parties to be strategic and careful in their choices. When a party is naturally favored by the context, there is less need or pressure to be strategic. As a result, we believe local party activity will have larger effects in the former contexts. As described in greater detail in chapter 3, parties are likely to be more strategic in their allocation of resources and energy in contexts where they need all the help they can get. When dominant, there is less pressure to be efficient.

To more explicitly capture these contextual effects, we estimated models that contained a three-way interaction between local party activity, party, and the statewide competitive context. The latter variable is a three-category variable based on the average statewide Democratic presidential vote for Gore in 2000 and Kerry in 2004. States in which this average vote was less than 0.5 standard deviations below the mean were coded –1 and deemed *favorable* for Republicans and *unfavorable* for Democrats. States where the vote was greater than 0.5 standard deviations above the mean were coded 1 and deemed *favorable* for the Democrats and *unfavorable* for the Republicans. States where the Gore-Kerry vote was between these values (i.e., between 0.5 below and above the mean) were coded 0 and are described as *competitive*. By this approach roughly one-third of the Democratic state parties fall into the unfavorable, competitive, and favorable categories, while only one-quarter of Republican parties in the dataset are in unfavorable contexts where activity appears to matter most, with 35% in unfavorable and about 40% in competitive contexts.[3]

Table 4.2 (p. 86) presents the results of these three-way interaction models. Though the activity index and the related interactions are not significant in the partisan registration model, the interaction effects are clearly evident in the three other models. To make these interactions more inter-

Table 4.2. The Influence of Local Party Electoral Activity on Election Outcomes: Three-Way Interaction with Activity, Party, and Competitive Context

Fixed Effects	Own Party Registration	Own Party Turnout	Presidential Vote	House Vote
Constant	41.646	21.267	39.159	49.908
Party	−19.490***	6.279***	17.373***	−8.848*
	(3.623)	(1.681)	(2.325)	(4.082)
Urban %	.049*	−.020	.054***	.044
	(.023)	(.010)	(.014)	(.025)
X Party	−.094**	−.095***	−.145***	−.139***
	(.035)	(.016)	(.022)	(.039)
Median Income $1000s	−.194***	−.067**	−.218***	−.251***
	(.041)	(.022)	(.028)	(.053)
X Party	.320***	.261***	.370***	.520***
	(.062)	(.033)	(.044)	(.080)
% Bachelor's Degree	.116	.436***	.508***	.403***
	(.078)	(.038)	(.049)	(.092)
X Party	.002	−.524***	−.909***	−.581***
	(.127)	(.060)	(.082)	(.147)
Activity	.096	.081	.314**	.154
	(.188)	(.072)	(.106)	(.167)
X Party	.145	.061	−.091	.049
	(.223)	(.098)	(.137)	(.236)
Context	−.768	7.415***	11.610***	14.401***
	(3.584)	(1.178)	(1.780)	(2.714)
X Party	−4.782	−15.945***	−26.308***	−33.952***
	(3.692)	(1.466)	(2.084)	(3.523)
Activity x Context	.081	−.681***	−1.002***	−.394*
	(.474)	(.182)	(.258)	(.197)
Activity x Party x Context	.005	.468***	.687***	1.195***
	(.300)	(.118)	(.165)	(.284)
Random Effects				
Between State Variance	113.232	11.739	33.482	52.348
Within State Variance	123.600	52.956	101.386	319.290
Activity Slope Variance	.290	.035	.115	.114
Activity-Intercept Covariance	−4.313	−.365	−1.967	−1.428
Observations	591	1182	1182	1181
Groups	27	48	48	48

Note: Fixed effects entries are unstandardized regression coefficients; standard errors are in parentheses; *p<.05; **P<.01; ***P<.001.

pretable, we calculated simple slopes for the activity index variable among the various combinations of party and competitive context. These simple slopes are presented in table 4.3 and displayed graphically in figures 4.1, 4.2, 4.3, and 4.4 (pgs. 88–89). Overall, the results show the decreasing impact of activity as the context becomes more favorable.

First, consider the effect of activity on presidential vote share, as shown in figure 4.1. For both parties, activity levels have zero impact in favorable contexts. Thus, variations in local Republican party activity in Alabama, for instance, do not correspond to variations in the local vote share of the parties' presidential candidates in 2008. However, in competitive contexts—Virginia, for example—there is a correspondence between activity and vote share for both parties. In unfavorable settings, the effect is even greater. So, Democratic activity in states like Alabama is strongly associated with better electoral performance. The simple slope, which is similar for both parties, suggests a substantial impact in unfavorable contexts: for every additional activity, vote share increases around 0.6% points. While this effect is not enough to change the outcome in unfavorable contexts, it may enhance future party prospects in these environments; the only way to make an unfavorable context favorable (or at least competitive) is to work to increase vote share. Furthermore, these efforts force the other party to expend resources in these unfavorable contexts, something they do not appear to do very

Table 4.3. Simple Slopes for Three-Way Interaction with Activity, Party, and Competitive Context

	Unfavorable	Competitive	Favorable
Presidential Vote			
Democrats	.628 (0.146)***	.314 (0.106)**	−.001 (0.182)
Republicans	.596 (0.203)**	.223 (0.113)*	−.150 (0.156)
House Vote			
Democrats	.547 (.235)*	.154 (.167)	−.240 (.280)
Republicans	1.004 (.331)**	.203 (.184)	−.599* (.251)
Own Party Registration			
Democrats	.011 (.320)	.097 (.188)	.182 (.288)
Republicans	.331 (.354)	.241 (.201)	.151 (.308)
Own Party Turnout			
Democrats	.294 (.102)**	.081 (.072)	−1.133 (.123)
Republicans	.396 (.141)**	.142 (.788)	−.112 (.108)

Note: Simple slopes are calculated from models in Table 4.2; standard errors are in parentheses; *p<.05; **P<.01; ***P<.001.

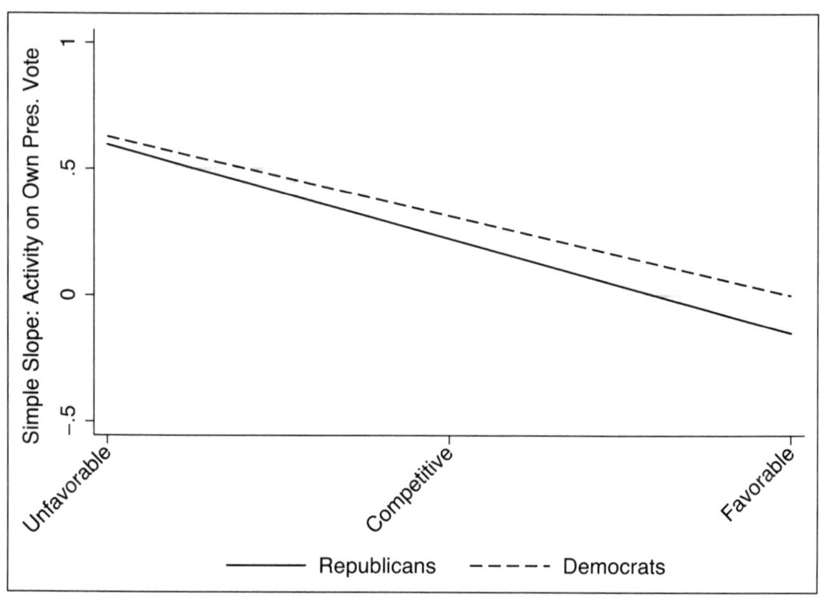

FIGURE 4.1. The Influence of Activity on Own Presidential Vote, by Party and Competitive Context

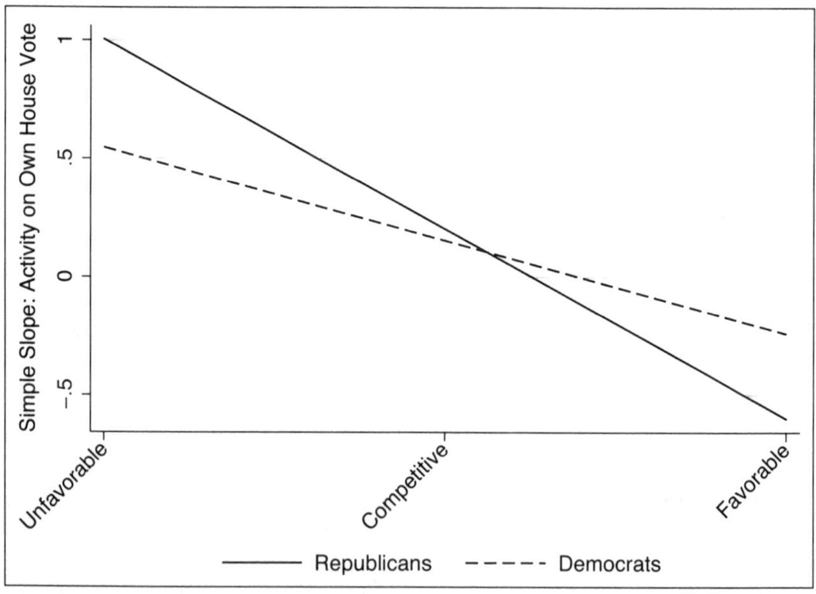

FIGURE 4.2. The Influence of Activity on Own House Vote, by Party and Competitive Context

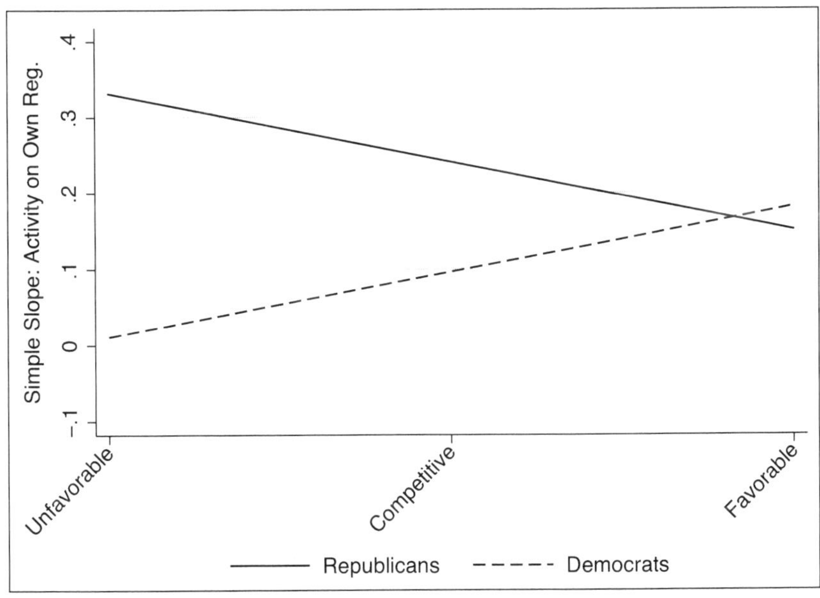

FIGURE 4.3. The Influence of Activity on Own Party

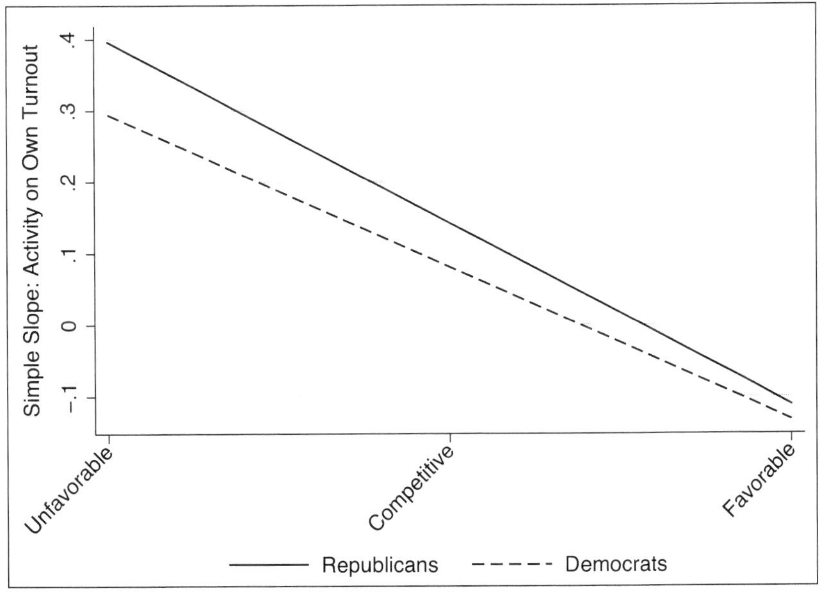

FIGURE 4.4. The Influence of Activity on Own Party Turnout, by Party and Competitive Context

efficiently. Indeed, this was at the heart of the Democratic 50-state strategy: to enhance Democratic fortunes in less favorable environments and to force the Republicans to compete everywhere, thereby diluting their resources.

Similar patterns emerge with the House vote model, as shown in figure 4.2, except the activity-context interaction differs much more between the parties. The pattern for Democrats resembles the presidential vote model: zero effect in favorable contexts, mild effects in competitive contexts, and substantial effects in unfavorable contexts. For Republicans, however, the contextual effects are even more pronounced. In unfavorable contexts, there is a 1:1 relationship between activities and vote percentage. Each additional activity boosts the local Republican House vote share by 1% point. However, this effect drops sharply in competitive states, and in favorable contexts the effect drops so far it becomes negative and statistically significant.

The partisan registration model, as shown in figure 4.3, fails to turn up a significant relationship in any scenario, which coincides with the findings from table 4.2. The partisan turnout model, however, looks similar to the vote models. Here, though, activity boosts turnout only in unfavorable contexts, as figure 4.4 reveals. In this context, an increase of about three or four activities is associated with an increase of 1% in the partisan turnout rate. In competitive states, the effect is still positive, though not significant. In favorable contexts, the slope is slightly negative although again not significant.

The findings from the three-way interaction models help to make sense of the initial negative findings for Republican activity. Activity matters much less in favorable contexts, especially for Republican parties. And, in the dataset, there are more Republican parties from favorable contexts than there are Democratic parties.[4] These conditions obscured the impact of Republican activity.

What explains the mediating impact competitive context has on the effects of local party activity? The data do not permit a definitive answer, but some possibilities seem likely. First, as alluded to previously here and in chapter 3, the incentives for strategic organizational behavior are reduced in favorable contexts. Party activity is a product of political actors attempting to get something from the resources they provide or corral. These transactions are varied in nature, but most commonly we expect resources to be provided in the hopes that election outcomes will be swayed. In a favorable context, where the party's candidates are already likely to be electorally successful, resource providers may be less concerned with affecting elections, because most outcomes will already be in the bag. Under these conditions, the distribution of party resources, and the corresponding activity levels, will reflect other objectives political actors may have, such as securing access or purposive benefits. It's not that fewer resources are available—in fact, there will likely be more in favorable contexts—but they are not distributed in a way that is strategic for the goal of boosting vote shares, an issue we discuss in greater detail in chapter 5.

In competitive or unfavorable environments, parties are hungrier because increasing vote shares may have meaningful effects on who gets elected. Even in highly unfavorable contexts, the resources that are available will be used shrewdly for electoral gain since no other benefits can accrue until the party improves its position. So, outside of favorable contexts, resource allocation should be more strategic and higher activity levels ought to correspond with bigger electoral shares, as we observed.

It is also possible that part of the interaction effect of context is due to a sort of ceiling effect caused by diminishing marginal returns. In favorable contexts, it may simply be the case that candidates of the dominant party are performing as well in elections as can be expected, since resources are ample. As a result, marginal increases in resources and subsequent party activity may not produce the same kinds of gains seen in less favorable contexts.

Different Activities, Different Effects

Overall activity levels are an indicator of vitality and organizational strength and directly reflect the commitments of various political actors to donate their time, money, and other resources to the local party organization. But it is possible that the effects found in the prior section of this chapter may reflect some activities more than others. Some of these activities may be focused around fundraising, such as assistance with fundraising or contributing money to candidates—the kinds of activities Frendreis and Gitelson (1999) label "adaptive brokerage" and that are captured in our fundraising sub-index. Other activities may be targeted toward voters, like canvassing or running GOTV efforts, which are captured in our grassroots index. In addition to possible variation in effects across the types of activities, there may be variation in the impact within these indexes. For instance, Gerber and Green (2000) find that turnout is increased substantially by personal canvassing but not by telephone calls, two activities that are captured in our grassroots index. Thus, it is worthwhile to disaggregate overall activity levels into sub-indexes and individual activities to better understand these effects. In this large array of possible actions local parties might take to influence election outcomes, which matter most?

Answers to this question can be complicated to analyze and even more difficult to present. In addition to the interaction effects among party, activity, and competitive context already identified, the models for each of the four dependent variables must now encompass four sub-indexes or 22 separate independent variables. Consider each activity individually, and one risks identifying a spurious relationship. Include all 22 variables in a single model, and the multicollinearity almost assures important relationships will be obscured. The same is true for the indexes.

Our approach first holds constant the moderating impact of competitive context by excluding those cases in favorable contexts. For the remaining cases (in unfavorable and competitive contexts), we ran 26 multilevel models for each dependent variable: one for each index and one for each of the activities, with control variables for urbanization, income, and education. Rather than running full interaction terms for party, we have simply split the sample into Democrats and Republicans.

The results are presented in table 4.4. The tables are organized first by dependent variable and then by party; the regression coefficients for each index and activity variable are presented (note the regression coefficient comes from a multivariate model, though for purposes of simplicity, the coefficients for the control variables are not presented). To ease the presentation and make the patterns more apparent, only significant relationships are displayed.

The first element of the table that jumps out is the relative paucity of significant relationships among Republican parties with respect to vote shares—and this is true even while parties in favorable contexts have been excluded. Only seven of the 52 activity variables across the vote outcome models are significantly related to election outcomes for Republicans. This is not completely surprising, given the earlier findings of this chapter. But it highlights the extent to which local Democratic committees influence election outcomes through their activities in ways the Republican committees do not. This may simply reflect the fact that there is more "slack" in Democratic electorates—more potential to mobilize the faithful and persuade partisans on the fence. The more affluent and better-educated Republican electorates, having more electoral resources (Brady, Verba, and Schlozman 1995), may present less opportunity to be influenced.

However, Republican grassroots activities do have significant and positive relationships with partisan registration and turnout. The registration effects seem to be due to two key individual activities for the Republicans— telephone campaigns and get-out-the-vote drives. The former result seems to add a caveat to Gerber and Green's findings; while telephone campaigns

Table 4.4. The Effect of Activity Sub-Indexes and Individual Activities on Electoral Variables

	Presidential Vote		House Vote		Partisan Registration		Partisan Turnout	
	Democrat	Republican	Democrat	Republican	Democrat	Republican	Democrat	Republican
Grassroots Sub-Index	.828					1.083		.640
	(.272)					(.512)		(.266)
Communications Sub-Index	1.040							
	(.319)							
Fundraising Sub-Index	.953							
	(.379)							
Internet Sub-Index	.648							
	(.301)							
Canvassing	2.809							
	(1.014)							
Campaign Events	4.170		4.967				2.357	
	(1.087)		(1.919)				(.863)	
Fundraising Events	3.626							
	(1.072)							
	(.851)							
Online Fundraising	2.890							
	(1.088)							
Assisted Online Fundraising Mailings								
Campaign Literature	2.735							
	(1.209)							

continued on next page

Table 4.4. *Continued.*

	Presidential Vote		House Vote		Partisan Registration		Partisan Turnout	
	Democrat	Republican	Democrat	Republican	Democrat	Republican	Democrat	Republican
Telephone Campaigns						3.454		
						(1.718)		
Billboard Space								
Posters or Lawn Signs	2.462							
	(1.154)							
Contributed Money				4.197				
				(2.101)				
Coordinated	3.088	2.834		5.501				
Campaigns	(.898)	(1.221)		(2.151)				
Registration Drives	2.534	2.607						
	(.966)	(1.186)						
Surveys								
Press Releases	1.871							
	(.878)							
Newspaper Advertising	3.146	3.114	4.754	3.983	3.677			
	(.884)	(1.126)	(1.555)	(2.005)	(1.565)			
Radio/TV Time	2.215							
	(1.106)							
Email Publicity								
Website Publicity								
Social Media Publicity								
Coordinated PACs								
GOTV	2.904			5.186		4.091		
	(1.043)			(2.442)		(1.766)		

Note: Entries indicate the unstandardized regression coefficient (and standard error) for the activity variable in a model including control variables (Y = activity + urbanization + median income + education); each activity variable was included individually in separate models. Only coefficients significant at the .05 level are displayed. Only cases in unfavorable and competitive contexts are included.

may not be successful in increasing turnout levels, here they are successful in increasing Republican registration rates. Given advance registration requirements in many states, it may be that a simple phone prompt from a local Republican committee may be sufficient to induce the more affluent and educated Republican electorate to do their civic duty and register to vote.

Another striking pattern is the sheer variety of Democratic activities that correspond with the local presidential vote. All four of the indexes and 12 of the 22 activities are significantly related to presidential vote share in the multivariate models. In contrast, only three Republican activities are significant in the presidential vote models, and only two Democratic activities are significant in the House vote models. It is possible this finding reflects the unusual dynamics of the 2008 Obama campaign. The Obama campaign developed a very extensive and robust grassroots operation in 2008. To the extent the campaign organization integrated their efforts with, and relied upon, local party organizations for some of this work, we would expect to see prominent local party effects for the Democrats in 2008. Indeed, FEC records reveal Obama's campaign transferred over $32 million to state and local party committees in the 2008 election; McCain's campaign transferred only $18 million. We might expect that higher levels of coordination and integration went along with these funds as well. All of this should have resulted in higher levels of activity among Democrats, which, as we reported in chapter 3, was true for some activities, particularly those involving the grassroots. But, more importantly, this money may have been focused more intelligently to maximize its impact.

It is also worth noting that none of the internet-based activities seem to have had much impact. Though there are some significant correlations between the electoral variables and campaign publicity through website, email, or social media, none of the relationships remain significant in the multivariate models that include controls for local demographics. Internet campaigning may get all the buzz, but it fails to deliver, at least for local party organizations.

In contrast, many of the old-school activities have the biggest impact. Fundraising events or other campaign events, like rallies and parades, were particularly important for the Democrats, with consistent and often very large effects. Telephone campaigns were one of the few helpful activities for Republicans—in this case, for partisan registration.

Among these traditional activities, the surprising standout was newspaper advertising. It was significantly related to Democratic registration rates and was significantly related to both presidential and House vote share—for *both* parties. Moreover, the effect sizes are remarkable. Republican House candidates did almost 4% points better in counties and towns where the Republican committee publicized the party and candidate through newspaper advertising. Democratic candidates did almost 5% points better when the Democratic committees took out newspaper ads. Presidential vote shares went up over 3% points for both parties. It is not obvious why we would observe such strong and consistent effects for newspaper advertising. The literature provides little help. Indeed, most work on campaign advertising focuses on TV ads, and studies of newspapers in the context of campaigns tend to look at reporting rather than paid advertising. We speculate that some of the impact may reflect the power of local, low-circulation newspapers, sometimes published weekly, that are common in smaller towns and cities. These papers are often focused on community affairs and local politics, and we suspect the readership is highly open to appeals made by parties on behalf of candidates. A Democratic chair in South Carolina described how the local party took out an ad in the weekly local newspapers listing all of the Democratic candidates, from president down to the local races, with an articulation of the party's accomplishments. Similarly, a local Democratic party in Maine put together a booklet that advertised the entire Democratic ticket as a slate and focused on each candidate on a separate page. The booklet was inserted into the local edition of the big daily paper in the region and then went into the local weekly papers. As a result, some voters may have received the booklet in their newspapers more than once.

National elected officials, even when residents of their district, probably are not familiar with all of these possible outlets in their districts, so having local party officials who have this knowledge may be extremely beneficial for them. It also helps explain why these effects are generally greater and more consistent for presidential candidates than for House candidates; House candidates presumably have more contacts in and knowledge of their districts, as they are smaller. It is less likely for presidential candidates to have this sort of knowledge about each county in the United States. From this view, presidential candidates would have greater need for on-the-ground operatives who have deep knowledge of the local context and who can be counted on as allies; local parties fit this bill. Clearly, though, this finding merits further investigation, especially considering the data indicate parties did less newspaper advertising in 2008 compared to 1980 (Roscoe and Jenkins 2014).

We saw in chapter 3 how local parties are heavily engaged in grassroots activities. The results in table 4.4 suggest this is prudent, though there are many qualifications. Certainly, these activities helped Obama in 2008—the Democratic models show significant effects for canvassing, distributing literature, running registration drives, and administering GOTV efforts. Even the placing of lawn signs was related to a bigger Obama vote share, which might surprise some party organizers who have always suspected lawn signs were more trouble than they were worth. As one Democratic chair put it, "We recognize to some extent we need to have the stupid lawn signs. And even as much work and trouble and source of complaints they are, you've got to have some." On the other hand, none of these activities were related to the Democratic House vote, and neither did they help Republican candidates, with one exception: GOTV drives were associated with a higher Republican House vote. As noted previously, they were also associated with Republican registration rates. But, they were not related—for either party—with the one outcome we might most expect: partisan turnout. Likewise, registration drives did not correspond to partisan registration rates for either party (though they did boost the presidential vote for both parties).

In general, then, it appears local parties can impact electoral outcomes using a variety of activities. Grassroots activities are the most consistently significant when looking at the indexes, but the analysis of the individual activities demonstrates that other activities like campaign events and newspaper advertising play a role in influencing registration, turnout, and vote totals.

Conclusion: The Continued Utility of Local Parties

Across the country, local parties engage in a variety of activities. Some of the activities are focused on assisting candidates, while others are focused on targeting voters. Regardless of the activity, though, they are generally undertaken with the understanding they will help the party achieve its goals, which are mainly electoral in nature. But this assumption—that local party activity matters—has never been adequately tested, particularly not in recent years. This is an important question because, if local party activity does not matter, then the central question guiding research into local parties should be why they exist and persist. But activity does matter, and here we demonstrate when and where it matters. There is a closer connection between activity and outcomes in unfavorable and competitive conditions. Efforts in these environments are more likely to produce results and less likely to run into any natural ceiling that exists in environments that are more favorable to party activity. This is good news for local parties—what they do matters in particularly those places where the collective party could use the most help.

This places local parties in the thick of US electoral politics. They are on the ground, where activists are engaging with voters and candidates, working to enhance party prospects. Without these activists, national parties and politicians would certainly be worse off. Parties, then, continue to be useful organizations in the political system. Despite repeated threats to their continued vitality, they have adapted to the changing political environment, both nationally and sub-nationally. Different party forms emerge in different state and local political environments, and these different forms have differing impacts on election outcomes, depending on the context in which these contests take place. While we no longer live in the heyday of local party machines, their work is still relevant, and understanding how they operate is still important to understanding elections and election outcomes in the United States.

The Future of Local Party Organizations

As we look to the future, we end where we began—with great concern over the place of local party organizations. The demise of soft money due to BCRA and the flood of outside spending unleased by *Citizens United* have led many to bemoan the coming downfall of political parties. Observers fret that groups and individuals willing to spend vast amounts of money outside the control of candidates and parties will spell doom for party organizations. At the same time, the internet is revolutionizing campaign communications, much as TV did in the mid-20th century, and seemingly has the potential to again marginalize the parties in the campaign process. Additionally, the rise of activist groups more concerned with ideological purity than electoral payoff has given rise to even more questions about the continued utility and vitality of local party organizations. Like David Broder in the 1970s, contemporary journalists and analysts are once again making funeral arrangements for the political parties. Robert Reich (2014) has declared "parties irrelevant in the age of the super PAC." Martha Brock (2011) wonders if parties are "now irrelevant in the age of social media." Rush Limbaugh, bemoaning the Republican Party's failure to fully embrace the Tea Party agenda, pondered if he "could ever remember a time when a political party just made a decision not to exist, for all intents and purposes" (Kovacs 2013). As Yogi Berra would say, it's déjà vu all over again.

We are decidedly more optimistic about the future of American political parties and particularly about the prospects for local party organizations. As we highlighted in chapter 1, party organizations have faced seemingly insurmountable threats in the past—the loss of patronage, the secret ballot, direct primaries, the rise of mass media, McGovern-Fraser reforms—and have responded to these challenges. Despite these threats, party organizations have adapted to the changing political environment and managed to find their niche connecting political resources with those who would find them useful (Frendreis and Gitelson 1999; Gibson et al. 1985; Gibson, Frendreis, and Vertz 1989). And as we have demonstrated here, parties have responded to further changes in the political landscape in the 21st century, such as the loss of soft money and the rise of the internet. While local party committees are not as structurally mature as national or state party organizations, they are more structurally mature than they were in the past (Roscoe and Jenkins 2014). Variations in these structures reflect differences in the political environment in which these local organizations exist, confirming that local political parties are adaptive organizations. They continue to be active in electoral politics, particularly in those areas that require access to the most important resource under their control—committed volunteers. Furthermore, this activity matters.

But is there something about our current political environment that is unlike past political environments and that will finally prove fatal to local parties? We think not. We firmly believe that local political party organizations will continue to adapt as the political landscape changes. Why do we believe this? First, as we noted in chapters 1 and 2, state regulations encompass specific elements of party structure, and state party organizations often contain specific provisions for the existence, structure, and activity of local party organizations. While these laws and rules do not completely ensure that local party organizations will not become moribund, they certainly provide protection for local party organizations. It is hard to imagine state lawmakers voting to change the laws in ways that undermine party organizations—organizations with which they identify and upon which they depend. It is also difficult to imagine party activists and state party officials voting to change party rules in ways that undermine the vitality of local party organizations, as these organizations still remain useful to them. Thus, it does not seem likely that circumstances will arise that will lead rational political actors with a stake in political parties to pull the plug on the life support these rules and laws offer to party organizations.

Furthermore, elections will continue to provide regular feedback to these organizations and encourage self-reflection. Party organizations will continue to assess the extent to which the team can do better in the next election cycle and work to adapt to the changing world of electoral politics. It is hard to imagine party organizations throwing in the towel and ceding the political field to other organizations.

Despite our confidence about the future of local party committees, others do not see such a rosy future for political parties, so we think it is useful here to examine what some contemporary observers view as potential threats to the future of local party organizations. Finally, we conclude by examining party strategies to respond to the changing political environment in ways that cultivate local party organizations.

Purposive Benefits and Party Activity

The rise of the Tea Party clearly serves as a locus of concern about party organizations, particularly among Republicans. This movement creates such consternation because it is both part of and apart from the Republican Party. As Abramowitz (2011) has shown, the Tea Party movement is really the culmination of a rightward shift among Republicans. "Over the past three decades there has been a marked increase in the size of the activist base of the Republican Party—an increase that preceded the rise of the Tea Party movement" (Abramowitz 2011, 5). Others have shown that Tea Party supporters are really just very conservative individuals and lack a set of unique beliefs that differentiate them from very conservative non–Tea Party Republicans (Arceneaux and Nicholson 2012).[1]

One distinguishing feature of the Tea Party, though, is the unique sense of identity it invokes in supporters, along with the high levels of activism displayed among its members. Tea Party supporters see themselves belonging to a movement and find a sense of identity in the shared membership of this movement. Surveys have tended to ask about "support" for the Tea Party, but the Battleground Poll by George Washington University-Politico has asked more directly about identity and membership. In this poll, each likely voter was asked, "Do you consider yourself a part of or do you identify with the Tea Party movement?" In the eight surveys between May 2011 and January 2014, between 19 and 24% of likely voters said they did. More importantly, among this slice of the population, identification was intense. Among Tea Party identifiers, between two-thirds and three-quarters said they "feel strongly" about their identity and membership. In this sense, the Tea Party is its own tribe, even if it is part of the larger Republican tribe. There is overlap among these identities, to be sure, but Tea Party identifiers are a distinct subset of the larger conservative milieu. Not all conservative Republicans develop a Tea Party identity. Only 36% of Republicans and 32% of conservatives identify with the Tea Party. But, in contrast, those with a Tea Party identification do tend to have conservative views that fall squarely in the domain of the Republican Party. For this reason, they gravitate toward it and direct their efforts toward remaking it rather than crafting a new political organization, as we suggested in chapter 1.

And these efforts are notable. While Tea Party supporters are not very distinguishable from other conservative Republicans on the issues, they are clearly much more active politically (Abramowitz 2011; Rapoport, Dost, and Stone 2014). Tea Partiers are almost three and a half times as likely to attend a rally or meeting as other Republicans and over twice as likely to display a sign or bumper sticker (Abramowitz 2011). Similarly, the widely noted "enthusiasm gap" between Democrats and Republicans in the 2010 election was due entirely to the zeal of Tea Party Republicans (Rapoport, Dost, and Stone 2014).

These shifts—the rightward movement of the Republican Party and the growing activism of the Tea Party on its fringe—have changed the nature of the Republican Party. "The most active segment of the Republican base almost doubled in size between the 1980s and 2000s and . . . also became considerably more conservative during this time period" (Abramowitz 2011, 6). This is significant because it has historically been the Democrats who were able to rely on grassroots efforts. Republicans, conventional wisdom held, drew strength from money and Democrats from numbers. And the Democratic establishment had to contend with its activist wing (e.g., the 1968 DNC Convention) in ways the Republican establishment did not. Social movements of the 20th century were almost always on the left. In the 21st century, it is the Republican base that is bubbling with grassroots energy.

Dealing with a vibrant but change-oriented base might be viewed as a "good problem" for the Republican Party establishment, were it not for the aggressive willingness of the Tea Party movement to pull Republican candidates to the right in nomination contests, often to struggle or lose in the general election. Their approach to electoral politics has been to back exceptionally conservative candidates in primaries through endorsements, activism, and campaign contributions. In 2010, the first election cycle in which they played a role, they backed 129 House candidates and 9 Senate candidates (Arceneaux and Nicholson 2012; Williamson, Skocpol, and Coggin 2011). However, while many of these candidates went on to win in the general election, a number of Tea Party candidates lost in more centrist states and districts to Democrats with beliefs more attuned to voters' preferences. For example, in 2010, Tea Party efforts almost certainly cost the Republicans Senate seats in Colorado, Delaware, and Nevada (Francia and Morris 2014; Williamson, Skocpol, and Coggin 2011), and in 2012, the Tea Party backed losing Senate candidates for races in Indiana and Missouri that would have been winnable for establishment Republicans (Francia and Morris 2014). In 2013, the Tea Party–backed Republican candidate for governor in Virginia lost as well to a Democrat who was not widely popular. Many have noted the difficulty the Tea Party movement caused Mitt Romney in 2012, when he was forced to tack right to compete with Tea Party favorites like Rick Santorum, Rick Perry, Herman Cain, Newt Gingrich, and Michele Bachmann.[2]

Why are these activists so willing to snatch defeat from the jaws of victory? And why do Republican party organizations bend so easily to their preferences? We believe the answers to these questions not only help us understand the nature of the Tea Party, but they also illuminate the nature of party activity in general.

Throughout the preceding chapters, we have focused most of our attention on the electoral goals of local party organizations. As we discussed in chapter 1, the activity of these organizations is the result of party organizers connecting available resources with the needs of other political actors and taking some form of profit. Historically, what other actors have wanted from local party organizations is help with electoral campaigns, and so most party activity over the course of American history has been directed at winning elections. As we saw in chapter 4, this activity can be helpful for candidates.

But it is important to point out that the "market exchange" resulting in party activity is not a perfectly efficient one, because not all party activity is directed at maximizing the electoral payoff. This can provide a challenge for political parties in that the central organizational focus of winning elections does not necessarily coincide with the goals of the organizers or those providing resources to those organizers. They may even be in opposition to one another.

This inefficiency occurs because party activity is as much supply driven as demand driven. What this means is that activity occurs not just because candidates request from parties exactly what they think will be useful (the demand), but also because donors and activists enable activity that will provide benefits to them (the supply). This is true historically and is true today.

For this reason, it is important to fully understand the nature of these benefits in order to understand how this is a challenge for local party organizations. As we outlined in chapter 1, both party organizers and activists derive material, solidary, and purposive benefits from party activity. While material benefits may play some role in motivating party organizers today, their importance has shrunk significantly from the days of party machines and patronage, and they are likely even less important for the rank-and-file activists. Solidary benefits continue to be important, particularly for activists. However, there are many organizations that provide solidary benefits—party organizations have nothing unique in this regard.

What really drives party organizers and activists today, we believe, are purposive benefits. But what, exactly, is meant by purposive benefits? There are two key components. First, purposive benefits involve the values, principles, or convictions of the individual, and, second, they connect these in a meaningful way to the goals and activities of the organization. Without some personal convictions, purposive benefits are impossible. If one has no beliefs about what is just or desirable in politics and government, then no purposive benefits can be derived from political activity. Conversely, the stronger and more intense those beliefs, the more benefits can be derived.

But these benefits only arise when the individual is acting in ways that further some *organizational* end that supports the individual's beliefs and convictions. Thus, purposive benefits "derive in the main from the stated ends of the association"—they involve the "suprapersonal goals of the organization" (Clark and Wilson 1961). In other words, individuals derive benefits by working for group goals that align with and further their own value and principles. However, as Salisbury (1969) points out, this formulation leads to a collective action problem, a challenge for all organizations and party organizations as well. The rational individual will understand that his or her contribution to the group effort is unlikely to make any difference to the group's efficacy, and so there will be strong incentives to free ride. People want their candidate to win the election, but it is hard to convince them to get out and volunteer to ensure that will happen.

Salisbury solves this problem by reformulating purposive benefits as primarily *expressive* in nature. Individuals derive benefits from the expression of their values, as "the action involved gives expression to the interests or values of a person or group" (1969, 16). Action is a form of expression, and a powerful one. There are many hackneyed expressions conveying our understanding that "actions speak louder than words," that "talk is cheap," and that you have to "put your money where your mouth is" and "stand up for what you believe in."

In addition to this expressive dimension, purposive benefits also have a *tribal* dimension. This dimension is explained well by social identity theory, which maintains that people have a deep-seated need to forge identity and do so in large part by defining groups to which they belong and opposing groups that are external (Tajfel and Turner 1986; Turner and Tajfel 1979). From this perspective, humans are fundamentally social animals, with a hardwired tendency to wrap their identity around in-group and out-group conceptions. We find our identity as members of a tribe. Actions that support one's own group, or that derogate the out-group, are important for helping to establish and maintain a needed sense of personal identity.[3] These tribal benefits differ from solidary benefits in that the latter are more about interpersonal relationships and social interaction. Clark and Wilson (1961, 135) note that solidary benefits are "independent of the precise ends of the association." Tribal benefits, in contrast, are about identity and the values, principles, and symbols that establish it—principles that are exemplified by the organization's goals and purposes.

Both expressive and tribal benefits are easily derived from activity in local party organizations. Expressive benefits can accrue from many kinds of activities, of course, and in an age of social media and blogging, it is easy for those with strong convictions to have their say. But opportunities for expressive *action* are harder to come by. Interest groups are typically remote, though some groups, such as the NRA, have local chapters that provide an outlet for group activity beyond paying membership dues. Groups that are local tend to be neutral, nonpolitical, or focused on local issues. While local issues can become heated, these heated issues do not necessarily fall along partisan or ideological lines, hence the old saying there's not a Democratic or Republican way to pave a street.

But local parties are almost always proximate. Party meetings are held in the community. Canvassing takes place in one's own neighborhood. Moreover, parties are a great nexus for expressive action because the two parties in the United States must take positions across a great variety of issues, making it likely people will find some connection to their most intensely held personal beliefs and principles. And these issues do tend to be heated, partisan, and ideological, invoking those expressive and tribal benefits in ways that other local organizations do not. Thus, the local party committee is often the only game in town.[4]

Similarly, local parties provide an outstanding opportunity to work for a tribe. Recent research has reconceptualized party identification as a specific example of broader social identity processes (Green, Palmquist, and Schickler 2002; Greene 2004; Roscoe and Christiansen 2010). For many, the parties are their tribes. It is not surprising, then, that for some there is great benefit in coming out for the local party organization and providing time and effort toward party goals. It helps cement and maintain personal identity.

Both expressive and tribal benefits share one important feature: they follow directly from the action of the individual, not the consequences of the action. Working for the party is, in itself, enough to convey the benefits to the activist. In other words, party activity need not have an actual impact on elections or the broader political process for it to provide benefits to those doing party work. To a significant degree, party work is symbolic, not instrumental. Party work allows people to express their values and reify membership in their political tribe, and it is this selective facet of the work that provides the benefit, not the collective aspect. Now, to be sure, the activity probably has some plausible connection to the party goals of electing its candidates, but activists are unlikely to look very seriously at this connection because the primary value of the action serves their own interests. This creates a different problem than the free-rider problem for party organizations; now they have a committed supply of volunteers, but it is difficult to direct them to focus solely on the organizational goal of winning. Unlike a business, which can fire a recalcitrant employee, there is little a local party committee can do with someone who keeps showing up to volunteer for local party activities, such as canvassing, and who does not toe the "party" line.

It is worth noting that individuals with an interest in accruing these kinds of purposive benefits are widely distributed geographically and may reside in areas where party competition is quite low. If party activity were purely instrumental and focused on collective party goals, no one would volunteer for party activity in these areas. But they do; as we saw in chapter 3, competition has a surprisingly modest relationship with party activity. More competitive areas have slightly higher levels of party activity, as we might expect if parties are deploying resources strategically toward collective goals, but the relationship is quite weak.

This may be because, as Shea (2014) has pointed out, there are reasons to expect a countervailing effect. Low competition is usually the result of ideological homogeneity in the local context, and this uniformity of opinion both reflects and amplifies needs for expressive and tribal action. In the deepest red and deepest blue counties in the most red and blue of states, there are plenty of committed individuals willing to do party work in support of candidates virtually assured of victory or defeat. Our data bear this out. For example, while 75% of the party organizations in the most competitive half of counties conducted canvassing efforts, fully 60% did in the lower half. Even in the 10% of counties that were the least competitive, almost half—47%—engaged in canvassing.

As a result of these dynamics, party activity is inefficient. From the perspective of the party's candidates, the party's resources, especially its activists, should be deployed strategically across the country in races where the effort may help to make the difference in who wins. To some extent this happens, particularly in states where a strong and effective state party leadership and an effective organizational culture allow for such coordination and targeting. But, because parties are relatively decentralized, party activity will bubble up where it will, dispersed across various areas and reflecting the local supply of activists as much as the demand from the party's candidates. For parties, this may be a mixed blessing. There are more available volunteers but not necessarily where the party leaders want them or in the mold that they would choose.

Furthermore, there is reason to expect that this supply of activists has bloomed in recent years with important shifts in party identification. These shifts, displayed here in sparklines using American National Election Study (ANES) data, are complicated. Between 1952 and 2008, each category of the party identification scale used in the ANES has traced a different trend. First, there has been a steady decline in the percentage of weak partisans: . Conversely, the percentage of leaners has continued to rise over the entire time period: . In contrast, the number of pure independents rose through the 1970s but has declined since then: . Finally, the percentage of strong partisans dropped sharply through the 1960s and 1970s but has rebounded considerably: . Hitting a low point of 23% in 1978, it rose to 33% by 2002.

The increasing share of strong partisans, along with the shrinking percentage of independents, has resulted in a slight strengthening of party identification overall. If the four-category scale is treated as interval level and a mean is calculated for each year, the data reveal a steady increase from 2.66 in 1978 to a high of 2.91 in 2002; it has remained high since, at 2.85 in 2008: . Even the rise of the leaners may suggest stronger partisanship, insofar as leaners' attitudes and behaviors tend to be more engaged and more consistently partisan than weak partisans (Keith et al. 1992). Although partisanship is still weaker today than in the 1960s, the dealignment bemoaned by Broder in the early 1970s has subsided to some degree.

Moreover, there is evidence that partisanship has become more closely aligned with ideology. Republicans have become more consistently conservative and Democrats more consistently liberal. Figure 5.1 (pg. 108) displays these changes. The percentage of Democrats (including leaners) who are liberal has risen from 70% in 1972 to 88% in 2008. Similarly, the percentage of Republicans who are conservative went from a low of 52% in 1974 to a high of 76% in both 2006 and 2008. Within each tribe, there are fewer people who have moderate views or who are cross-pressured ideologically.

These changes are significant for our analysis of local party activity because they suggest there has been a greater alignment of expressive and tribal benefits. Not only has the number of individuals with strong connections to their party risen, but they are less likely to be cross-pressured,

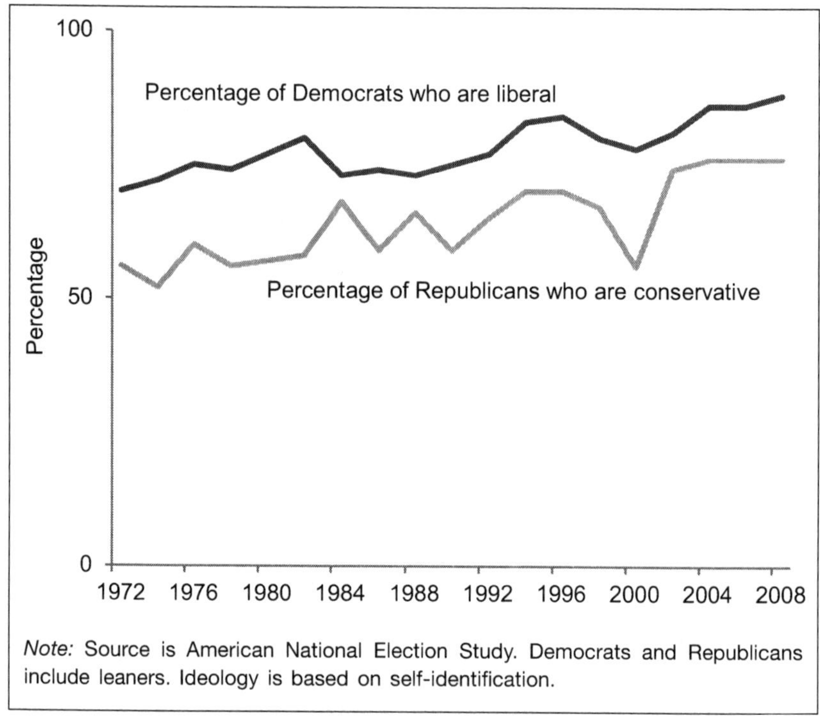

FIGURE 5.1. Ideological Polarization of Partisans

unlike the conservative Southern Democrat of the 1960s. Under these circumstances, it would be surprising if a greater supply of local party activists did not emerge.

Some evidence for this supposition is provided in figure 5.2, which graphs the average number of campaign activities in which Americans reported engaging in the surveys by the ANES. There were five options: influence the vote of others, attend political meetings/rallies, work for a party/candidate, display button/sticker, and donate. Of course, most Americans do none of these, so the means are low across the entire time period. But, what is clearly notable is the sharp increase in the 2004 and 2008 surveys. Moreover, 2002 was the first midterm in the data series for which campaign participation had risen compared to the prior presidential election. It is clear that Americans are participating more in recent campaigns.

Now, these activities need not involve local party organizations. But the evidence suggests they do. When the data on local party activity from

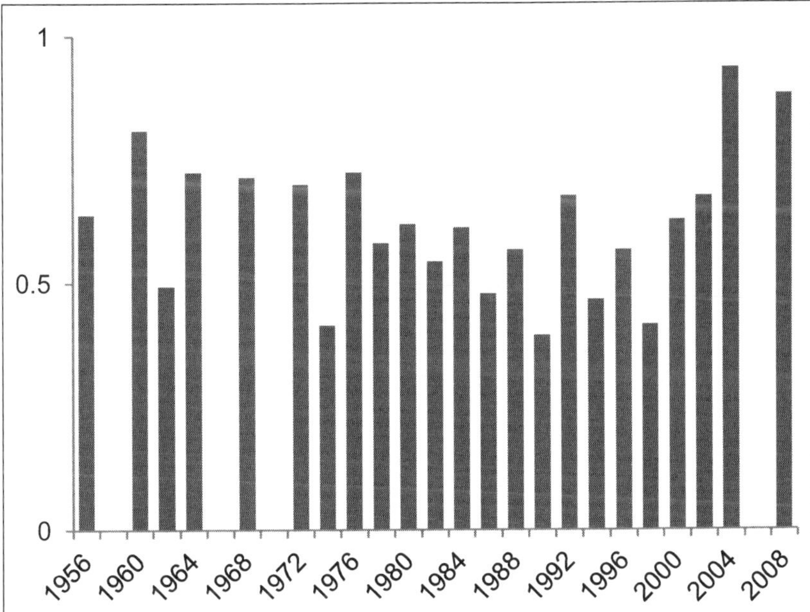

Note: Source is American National Election Study. Figures represent the average number of political activities respondents reported engaging in, out of five possible activities (influence the vote of others, attend political meetings/rallies, work for party/candidate, display button/sticker, donate).

FIGURE 5.2. Levels of Political Activity

2008 are compared to comparable data from the 1990s and 1980s, clear trends toward increasing grassroots activity are evident (Roscoe and Jenkins 2014). Furthermore, the percent of respondents reporting in the ANES that they had been contacted by political parties has increased from 19% in 1990 to over 42% in 2008. Of course, not all of this contact comes from local organizations, but taken as a whole the data suggest increasing party activity at all levels. For parties then, this is good: there is an increasing supply of committed workers to provide more boots on the ground. But this can also pose a challenge to national and state organizations in the party network, as these boots on the ground cannot be guided in the same way they can be in other organizations (such as the military, where the phrase "boots on the ground" originated).

From this perspective, the Tea Party movement is just a highly vis-ible manifestation of the natural party exchange market and a reflection of broader trends in political attitudes and behavior. Part of what is supplying Tea Party energy and making the movement notable is the heightened degree to which these individuals receive purposive benefits from political action. This group of people seems to hold their opinions with particular fervor and appears equally to enjoy expressing them. This is clear from an analysis of the self-identified Republicans (excluding leaners) in the 2012 ANES. While 70% of non–Tea Party Republicans report discussing politics with family or friends, 87% of Tea Party Republicans do. The former do so on average 2.2 days a week compared to 3.1 days for Tea Partiers. Tea Party Republicans also see themselves as more opinionated: 43% say they have somewhat more or a lot more opinions than the average person; only 23% of non–Tea Party Republicans feel this way. They also appear to have a greater sense of partisan identification. Among non–Tea Party Republicans, 44% call themselves "strong" Republicans; over 72% of Tea Party Republicans do so.[5]

The intense purposive and expressive satisfaction Tea Partiers derive from political action is evident in the zeal and spectacle of Tea Party rallies. These qualities were on display early in the movement's history, during the tax day protests in 2009, when over 750 "tea parties" were held across the country. Protestors decorated themselves with tea bags and tea pots, dressed in colonial garb, and held signs reading "Got Pork?," "Abolish the IRS," and "Honk If You Are Upset About Your Tax Dollars Being Spent on Illegal Aliens" (Robbins 2009). Other protestors held signs reading "The Pirates Are in DC"; chanted "give me liberty, not debt"; and blasted Twisted Sister's "We're Not Gonna Take It" from the PA system (Fox News 2009). A year and a half later, protestors gathered in DC with similar fanfare, toting signs with classic libertarian slogans like "Don't Tread on Me" along with more colorful takes on populism, such as the one that read "I may be a redneck, but I know how to balance a checkbook" (Somashekhar 2010). One protestor described the expressive nature of the movement, explaining that the Tea Partiers "think it's time the silent majority starts speaking up." Another felt encouraged by the tribal dimension of the rally: "It's nice to know we are part of something bigger" (Somashekhar 2010).

Given that the Tea Party movement combines the two key components of purposive benefits—expressive and tribal action—it is not surprising that it has drawn extensive support from this set of individuals. However, while Tea Partiers are opinionated conservatives with strong Republican identification, they also hold an identification with the Tea Party itself. This sets them apart from the traditional right wing of the Republican Party. Herein lies the challenge because the Tea Party is not necessarily interested in winning at all costs; they are more interested in supporting candidates who personify Tea Party beliefs.

These considerations explain the tensions between the Tea Party and establishment Republicans, who are much more willing to be pragmatic about elections. For these party insiders, then, the Tea Party movement must be seen as a mixed blessing. The organizational energy they provide is a wonderful resource, but their drive for purposive benefits can make it difficult for the party organizations to harness this energy in ways that are strategically helpful. This problem, however, is not fundamentally different than the problem faced by all party organizations that rely on local party activists, nor is it historically unique—parties have always faced these challenges. But in this context, the 50-state strategies of the two major parties and the state parties' focus on campaign training, which we focus on at the end of this chapter, make sense; they may be attempting to govern the ungovernable.

Money and Local Party Organizations

Of course, the argument can be advanced that these trends among activists are unimportant because money is the most important resource that candidates need, and parties have become more and more marginalized from the money game. From this perspective, local party organizations may be losing their utility. How much longer will they last in this era of big money elections dominated by new organizational forms that have emerged in recent years and that have taken over the money functions previously performed by parties? These organizations, which are involved primarily in campaign finance and which often straddle the line between interest group and party, emerged in the wake of BCRA in 2002, which eliminated the national parties' soft money accounts and forced big-money donors to find new ways to funnel money into the electoral process.

For these donors, the parties' soft money machines had been useful in the prior decade as a way to circumvent the regulated hard money contribution limits of the Federal Election Campaign Act (FECA). At the peak of soft money in 2000 and 2002, the parties together collected about $500 million in soft money, which was held in "nonfederal" accounts. During this period, federal law and Federal Election Commission (FEC) regulations permitted these unregulated contributions and expenditures in nonfederal accounts as long as they were limited to generic party building or issue advertising and did not engage in express advocacy for federal candidates. Of course, the parties were able to stretch the limits of "issue advertising" in ways that were certainly intended to influence federal elections. BCRA closed the parties' nonfederal accounts and thereby eliminated the soft money machines. It could not, of course, eradicate the desire among large donors to influence politics, elections, and policymaking. So, when the soft money went away, organizational entrepreneurs essentially created new organizations that would implement the same function. It is in these new organizations that observers see the greatest challenge to political parties, so it is worth examining them in some detail.

The original vehicle for this activity were organizations incorporated under section 527 of the nonprofit tax code. These groups, labeled "Political Organizations," are regulated only by the IRS and therefore fall outside the purview of the FEC and its regulations.[6] A 527 organization may not make contributions to candidates, parties, or other groups, and they may not engage in express advocacy that calls directly for support for or opposition to federal candidates. They can, however, engage in unlimited "issue advocacy" and can do so in ways that are almost certain to influence voters. This is the same type of advertising the parties engaged in using soft money. After BCRA eliminated soft money, spending by 527 committees rocketed up as donors shifted their soft money dollars into these groups' coffers. Data reported by the Center for Responsive Politics show federally focused 527s spent over $440 million in 2004, the first election after passage of the BCRA.

One of the earliest and most well-known examples of 527 organizations was the Swift Boat Veterans for Truth, which spent over $25 million during the 2004 presidential campaign on TV ads raising questions about the integrity of John Kerry's service in Vietnam. The ads never asked voters to oppose Kerry's bid for office, nor did they encourage voters to choose Bush. As a result, the ads were intended to be issue advocacy. In 2006, the FEC ruled that the group's activity did amount to express advocacy and sanctioned the group for not registering as a political committee and for not following the rules that applied to all PACs regarding the collection of contributions. However, the FEC dismissed claims from the Kerry campaign that Swift Boat Veterans were really coordinating with Bush and the Republican Party. Ultimately, the group paid a $300,000 penalty, but not until two years after Bush won the election.

Though Swift Boat Veterans were particularly noteworthy, they were not even among the top 527 spenders in 2004. The big 527 players were all on the Democratic side of the election: America Coming Together spent

$78 million, the Joint Victory Campaign spent $72 million, and the Media Fund spent $57 million. While these groups were created specifically to take advantage of the 527 rules, many longstanding interest groups created 527 affiliates, including Club for Growth (spending $12 million in 2004), Sierra Club (spending $6 million in 2004), and the National Association of Realtors (spending $3 million in 2004).

By 2008, 527 spending on politics largely had been displaced by 501c money, particularly that of 501c4 social welfare organizations. Under the tax law, 501c4 groups have several advantages over 527s. First, their donors can remain anonymous. Also, they can engage in express advocacy. Their main disadvantage for donors wishing to influence elections is that their primary activity must be the promotion of social welfare, not electoral politics. In practice, however, this has been interpreted widely as meaning less than half of their expenditures can be political. Even with this limitation, 501c4 funding exploded. In 2006, according to the Center for Responsive Politics, 501c4 groups spent just over $1 million; in 2012 they spent over $250 million. The first cycle to see significant 501c4 spending was 2010. In that election cycle, several big players emerged, the largest of which has been Crossroads GPS. This organization, which we discuss more fully later in this chapter, was founded by Republican strategists Karl Rove and Ed Gillespie. The group spent $17 million in 2010 and an astounding $71 million in 2012. Americans for Prosperity, bankrolled by the conservative billionaires Charles and David Koch, spent $37 million in 2012. Indeed, most of the 501c4 money has supported Republican candidates. Of the top ten 501c4 spenders in 2012, eight were conservative. The two liberal groups in this list, the League of Conservation Voters and Planned Parenthood, together spent only half of what Americans for Prosperity spent by itself. Overall, according to the Center for Responsive Politics, conservative 501c4 spending vastly outstripped liberal spending in 2012; the former spent $270 million and the latter only $59 million.

The timing of these tremendous increases in 501c4 spending was not arbitrary. Prior to 2010, even these groups labored under one major constraint that was put into place by BCRA. Under the electioneering communication provisions of BCRA, no group of any type could fund advertisements mentioning a federal candidate in the period preceding elections, unless it used contributions that were collected under FECA hard money source and amount restrictions.[7] In other words, just prior to elections only PACs could run election ads using their hard money contributions.

But this constraint was removed by the Supreme Court in its ruling in the *Citizens United* case in 2010. On the grounds of First Amendment free speech rights, the Court struck the electioneering communication provisions and thereby opened up the possibility of any group spending unlimited amounts of money from any source on elections. While there was a good deal of concern about the future of political parties with the elimination of soft money under BCRA, the real worries emerged with the flood of money that erupted after *Citizens United.*

Donors created a new vehicle for spending that has become known as a Super PAC, but which is legally a 527 committee that is regulated by the FEC as an Independent Expenditure Only Committee, to get around the tax law that still required 501c4 groups to spend no more than half their funding on elections. These Super PACs can collect money from any source in any amount and spend all of it on electoral politics.[8] According to the Center for Responsive Politics, 1,300 Super PACs emerged in the 2012 election and spent an astounding $600 million. American Crossroads, the Super PAC sibling of Crossroads GPS, spent $105 million by itself in 2012. Conservative billionaire Harold Simmons was a major contributor to American Crossroads, giving over $20 million directly and $3 million through his company, Contran Corporation. The donations to the top liberal Super PAC in 2012, Priorities USA Action, were smaller but still orders of magnitude larger than the direct contribution limits of FECA. Fred Eychaner, chairman of Newsweb Corporation, donated $4.5 million. The founder of Renaissance Technologies, James Simons, gave $5 million. Many others gave multimillion-dollar checks. And almost all of this money ended up funding express advocacy television campaign commercials.

There has still been growth in 501c4 spending, as well, because these organizations need not disclose their donors. This characteristic has spawned a new dynamic in campaign finance called dark money. Money flows among various nonprofit committees in ways that are difficult or impossible to track, requiring an examination of IRS reports as well as FEC records. Even then, the original individual donors may be kept secret. These dark money flows permit donors—including institutional donors—to fund extensive political activity through these organizations without having their identity revealed.

That affluent donors would seek to fund election campaigns is not surprising nor is it a new phenomenon. At least since the late 19th century, when Mark Hanna marshaled several million dollars to get McKinley elected, big money has had a prominent place in election campaigns. The rise of electronic media, particularly television, heightened the importance of money in elections. Of course, any individual or corporation can conceive, produce, and pay to broadcast an ad on its own, and sometimes they do. But, the organizational world has hatched a number of forms that help connect the desire of affluent donors to make a difference with the needs of candidates to have election advertising broadcast on their behalf.

Political parties have had some role in this, though it has been variable. This variability of the role of parties in campaign finance is a sign of their adaptability. Prior to FECA, donors could essentially give any entity—candidate, group, or party—any amount in campaign contributions. In early periods, the party was central. Hanna collected those millions of dollars for McKinley while serving as the chair of the Republican National Committee. But, in the candidate-centered milieu of the mid-20th century, that money typically went directly to candidates. For example, the big money backing Nixon's presidential bid in 1972 went to his Committee for the Re-Election of the President (CREEP), not the Republican party committees. Despite this and despite the passage of FECA, parties found a way to circumvent the spirit of the law with the rise of soft money. Once again, parties emerged as central players in financing elections, although candidates still played an equally important role to be sure. But BCRA took away this party "food" source, and *Citizens United* unleashed a whole slew of new organizational forms devoted to financing and influencing elections, a central role of parties. And yet, despite these challenges, we remain skeptical that these changes in flows of money signal the death knell for political parties for two key reasons.

First, many of these new groups are really party organizations to a significant degree. One main reason is that they are often headed by individuals with extensive histories within the major parties. The best examples are Crossroads GPS, the 501c4, and American Crossroads, the Super PAC. The former spent $70 million and the latter spent $105 million in 2012. Though neither group is incorporated as a party committee, they are managed by people who are fixtures in the Republican Party establishment. The founders are Karl Rove, who had served as George W. Bush's political director and consultant, and Ed Gillespie, former chair of the RNC. The president of both groups is Steven Law, who had served as chief of staff for Mitch McConnell, the Republican Senate Minority Leader, and as executive director of the National Republican Senatorial Committee. The leadership team of American Crossroads is full of party stalwarts. Chairman Mike Duncan had served as chairman and treasurer of the RNC. Director Jo Ann Davidson was the cochair of the RNC and chairman of the 2008 Republican National Convention. Political director Carl Forti played several roles at the National Republican Congressional Committee, including communications director. It is difficult to see Crossroads as anything but the independent expenditure arm of the Republican Party.

This is not an isolated example. Magleby's (2014) thoughtful analysis of the Super PAC universe identifies three categories of Super PACs: candidate-specific Super PACs that form solely to spend in support of a single candidacy, interest group-centered Super PACs that serve as independent expenditure arms of existing interest groups, and party-centered Super PACs like American Crossroads that support multiple party candidates and that often have connections to the party establishment. Among the 53 Super PACs that spent at least $1 million in 2012, only nine are party centered, but they spent $194 million and account for about one-third of all the spending among these key Super PACs.[9]

Among these party-centered groups, ties to the party are clear. Majority PAC, which spent $38.1 million, is founded by the former chief of staff to Harry Reid, the Democratic Senate Majority Leader. The founder and executive director of House Majority PAC, which spent $30.7 million, had worked in various roles at the Democratic Congressional Campaign Committee. Young Guns Action Fund is headed by individuals who had served as deputy chiefs of staff to Eric Cantor, Republican House Majority Leader.

Are these new groups separate from or part of the party? It is difficult to tell. On the one hand, they appear to be simple extensions of the political parties—new organizational appendages that are carrying on the soft money function that the national party committees had provided in the past. On the other hand, they lack any formal ties to other party committees—indeed, they are prohibited by law from coordinating with party or candidate committees. It is too early to tell if these new organizations are sui generis—or, more accurately in biological terms, a new species within the genus of political organizations—or simply adaptations of the political party form that have emerged in response to the changing environment. Only time will tell. But it is clear that these organizations are operating in concert with the political parties. Once the primaries are done and it becomes a question of "us" versus "them," these organizations line up behind the party nominee and give the other team their best shot. Importantly, these organizations are increasingly "taking one for the team." The negative advertising functions of campaigns that are almost universally disliked by voters but equally effective have been largely taken over by these organizations, leaving the candidates and the parties with much cleaner hands. So, for political parties, it is not entirely clear whether these new organizations are an invasive species or a symbiotic partner.

The second reason we remain skeptical that these dramatic shifts in the world of political money spell doom and gloom for local party organizations in particular is because local party organizations have not been central to the money game for a long time, if they ever were. It is tempting to presume the financial currents of elections have largely been diverted to other watersheds. If the new nonprofit money has replaced party money, it is reasonable to suppose that the new campaign finance regime has marginalized local parties. The data, however, tell a different story. At the national level, it is not so much that the money flows have been diverted as much as there has been a deluge of new money that has carved new waterways.

But local party spending was never more than a small stream anyway. Trends in campaign spending, displayed in figure 5.3, suggest local parties have played a consistent, if consistently small, role in the overall scheme of funding federal campaigns over the last decade.[10] First, it is important to note that local party spending has increased over this time period, more than doubling from 1996 to 2012 from $12 million to $27 million. However, this money has never been an important piece of the overall campaign

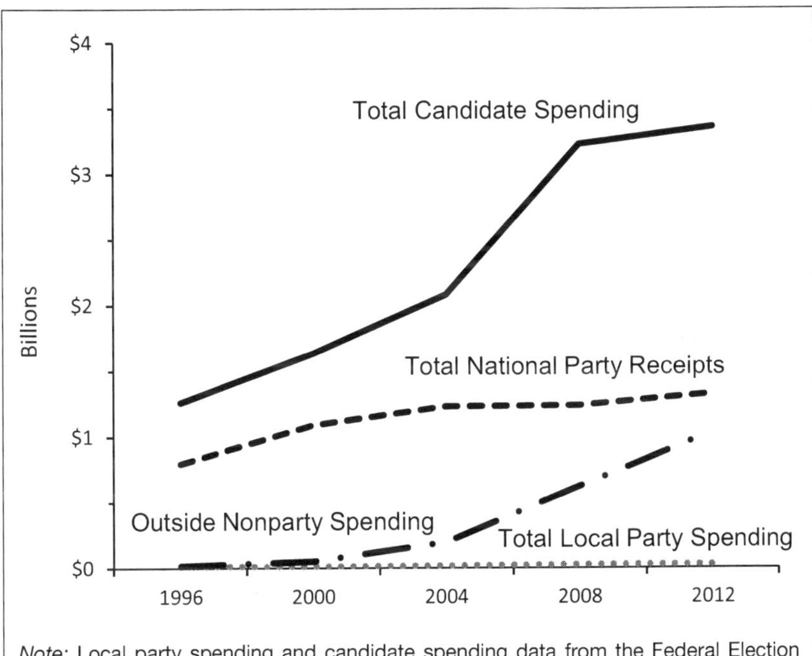

Note: Local party spending and candidate spending data from the Federal Election Commission; national party receipts data from the Campaign Finance Institute; outside nonparty spending data from the Center for Responsible Politics.

FIGURE 5.3. Campaign Finance Trends

finance picture. Local party spending is dwarfed by candidate disbursements, never totaling more than 1% of what candidates spend. It is meager compared to the fundraising of the national parties, too, never amounting to much more than 2% of what the six national committees raise. In the last two presidential elections, local parties spent around $27 million on federal elections. The Center for Responsive Politics calculates the total amount of spending by candidates, parties, and nonprofits was $5.3 billion in 2008 and $6.3 billion in 2012. Local party spending was virtually negligible in comparison, representing about 0.5% in both elections. As the campaign finance world shifted radically, the role of local parties changed little, mainly because they were never a key part of that world to begin with.

Most of the financial activity in the parties has always been at the national level. The rise of the nonprofits has not diminished the amount of money the national committees bring to elections—national party receipts have risen or stayed level year after year since 1996 (though it has been more level than rising during the last decade). The real problem for the national parties is that the rest of the campaign finance universe has exploded around them. Candidate spending and outside nonparty spending have jumped considerably over the last decade, far outstripping the meager gains in national party fundraising. In 1996, the national parties raised about $797 million, which equaled about 63% of the amount candidates raised and spent themselves. Over the years, this eroded to just under 40% in the last two presidential elections. Similarly, nonparty outside spending amounted to just under $18 million in 1996. National party committees spent far more on elections than these outside groups—44 times as much. In 2012, outside spending hit $1.04 billion, almost as much as the national parties spent.

While the new wave of outside money has begun to swamp national party spending, there has also been an important shift in the ways parties spend money, suggesting that parties are starting to adapt to this new environment. Put simply, parties at all levels are giving less directly to candidates and spending more on their own, either independently or in coordination with candidate campaigns. In 1996, data collected by Frendreis and Gitelson (1999) showed 78% of local Republican and 75% of local Democratic party committees contributed to candidates. By 2008, these figures fell to 59% and 57%. Similarly, the parties at all levels are giving less money to candidates than they had in the past. FEC data show contributions to candidates in 2012 were less than half of what they were in 1996, though in no year did these direct donations amount to much in the grand scheme of things.

A third reason contemporary campaign finance is unlikely to marginalize the parties is the expected effect of the Supreme Court's ruling in

McCutcheon v. FEC (2014). In this ruling, the Court struck the aggregate limits on individual contributions, meaning donors can now give to as many candidates, PACs, or party committees as they would like, though each donation must still fall below the cap on discrete contributions. As many have pointed out, including Justice Breyer in his dissent, this opens the door for massive coordinated contribution schemes involving numerous party committees. Party committees can already form joint fundraising committees that distribute large checks among all the committees in proportion to their contribution caps (donors can give no more than $32,400 to a national party committee and no more than $10,000 to a state or local committee in any year). Single donations to these joint fundraising committees had been limited by FECA's aggregate limit on total contributions to parties ($74,600 to all committees combined, $48,600 to sub-national party committees). Now these limits have been removed. Donors can now give the maximum to every party committee involved. Once distributed, these committees can simply transfer the funds back to the national committee. Thus, if a joint committee involves the three national committees and the 50-state committees, a donor can write a check for over $1 million to the DNC or the RNC every two-year election cycle. It's also possible to include local party committees in these joint fundraising committees, greatly increasing the amount of money that can be contributed to the parties and carving out a critical new role for local committees in the money game. It seems unlikely that donors and party organizers will not take advantage of these party schemes.

So the money landscape has changed, but the money landscape in politics is always changing. Parties adapted in the past, and there are signs that they continue to adapt. Where does this leave local political parties?

Conclusion: The Future of Local Parties

Throughout the preceding pages, we have presented data that show local parties are generally mature organizations, though not usually built to be active outside the campaign season; during these seasons, they are very active, particularly in some environments; and this activity can have a positive effect on the party's electoral fortunes. We also find evidence that local parties are heavily engaged in grassroots activities, even more so than 30 years ago. These shifting patterns of activity appear to represent these organizations' attempts to adapt to a changing environment.

In electoral politics in today's environment, there are two important resources: money and labor. As we argued earlier, local party committees have never really been involved in the money game. But local political parties have almost always been critical for providing campaign labor. And the current environment, with aligned partisan and ideological identities, has produced an increased supply of volunteers who receive purposive benefits from electoral politics and an increased need to mobilize the polarized bases. In this regard, the resources local parties broker are plentiful, even if party organizations are left with the challenge of governing the ungovernable.

At this critical nexus, with more volunteers who are more ideological, and with candidates and other organizations running the media show, there are signs that parties have begun, once again, to adapt. With their traditional food source, money, diminished, parties have shifted efforts to focus on another critical electoral food source: labor. As the portion of the electorate that is amenable to persuasion declines, the real game is about getting those who are already inclined to support you out to vote. Indeed, the focus on the ground game has rebounded to levels not seen since the glory of machine parties (Beck and Heidemann 2014, 261).

This focus extends to all levels. Local parties focus more now on labor-intensive electoral activities than in the past (Roscoe and Jenkins 2014). But we also see this with state and national parties. These organizations, which are increasingly spending money on their own as opposed to giving it to candidates, are also organizing the ground game. As we demonstrated in chapter 2, the most common form of assistance that state parties provide to local parties is campaign training. How might state party strategists channel the bubbling grassroots energy among their local activists? By providing opportunities to inform local organizers and volunteers about the best strategies and techniques to reach party goals.

Furthermore, national parties have developed 50-state strategies that focus on building organizational capacity and robust activity across all local electoral contexts. Candidates can build their own organizations, as Obama did in his initial campaign for the presidency, but maintaining the vitality of these organizations is difficult. Utilizing the existing local party apparatus is simply easier, and this is what the parties have sought to do. The Democratic 50-state strategy came first and focused on building Democratic organizations from the ground up in all states (DNC 2014). The Republicans responded in 2013. Both parties have focused these efforts on understanding local context and using local workers, which puts local party organizations at the center of these operations.

Are local party organizations under duress in the new political environment? To be sure. But will this new political environment finally lead to the extinction of political parties? We doubt it. Party organizations are hardy organizations. They may be no tardigrade, which lives on after being frozen, boiled, exposed to radiation, or sent into space, but they are certainly not going the way of the dodo any time soon. Party organizations will continue to adapt to the changing US political landscape, as they have done for centuries.

Local Party Chair Survey

Survey Responses

TABLE A.1. Survey Requests to Participate and Responses Received

	Democrats		Republicans	
	Requests	Responses	Requests	Responses
Alabama	42	12	56	15
Alaska	33	12	68	16
Arizona	14	5	13	2
Arkansas	0	0	6	3
California	56	32	45	13
Colorado	63	22	19	9
Connecticut	21	12	105	36
Delaware	4	1	0	0
Florida	40	13	51	19
Georgia	0	0	109	22
Hawaii	3	1	3	2
Idaho	37	16	42	15
Illinois	53	14	93	19
Indiana	86	23	37	7
Iowa	92	40	80	23
Kansas	8	2	87	12
Kentucky	67	13	88	24
Louisiana	4	0	0	0
Maine	16	2	15	5
Maryland	22	7	20	6
Massachusetts	223	76	73	23
Michigan	79	29	79	16
Minnesota	76	27	0	0
Mississippi	51	9	30	7
Missouri	0	0	0	0
Montana	42	15	55	10
Nebraska	49	12	0	0
Nevada	13	1	16	4
New Hampshire	12	7	10	5
New Jersey	17	5	12	0
New Mexico	21	4	32	10
New York	23	6	10	2
North Carolina	86	21	101	27
North Dakota	43	14	45	8
Ohio	22	6	75	17
Oklahoma	11	5	70	15

Oregon	16	9	35	10
Pennsylvania	31	10	0	0
Rhode Island	23	6	0	0
South Carolina	33	9	0	0
South Dakota	8	3	47	7
Tennessee	77	12	60	11
Texas	198	58	212	45
Utah	24	9	29	9
Vermont	14	6	12	2
Virginia	111	41	123	27
Washington	36	13	39	11
West Virginia	43	9	51	15
Wisconsin	66	19	60	15
Wyoming	20	8	0	0
Total:	2,129	676	2,213	544

Measuring Party Organizational Culture

As described in chapter 2, we measure the *effectiveness* of local party organizational culture; parties that score highly on these measures should function more effectively. Respondents were asked to indicate on a five-point scale their agreement with various descriptive statements (e.g., Local parties are encouraged to be creative and innovative). There are three items included to measure the seven attributes that make up our index of effectiveness, for a total of 21 questions. Table A.2 (p. 126) indicates how individual questions contribute to the various attributes that measure cultural effectiveness.

As the full text of the survey included in this appendix indicates, respondents were asked to indicate their agreement with a given statement on a five-point Likert scale. Individual questions that relate negatively to a specific attribute were reverse recoded such that they relate positively, with the result that all attributes take on higher values when the party culture is more effective. Our overall measure of cultural effectiveness was calculated by taking the average of all of 21 items.

For our analysis of organizational culture, the unit of analysis is the state party organization. In this case, the phenomenon of interest, conceptually speaking, should not have substantive variation across local parties, insofar as the state party organizational culture is a singular culture that overarches the entire party apparatus in the state. As a result, the responses from local party chairs cannot be viewed as a sample from which population

Table A.2. Questions Used for Organizational Culture Attributes

Attribute 1: Culture management	
This party rarely holds events designed to create a shared sense of direction and accomplishment.	−
This party has strong values which are widely shared by its members.	+
Party members lack a clear understanding of what its values and philosophies are.	−
Attribute 2: Innovativeness	
Local committees are encouraged to be creative and innovative.	+
Local parties are always encouraged to be flexible to changes in the external environment.	+
This is not an innovative organization, and new ideas about winning elections are generally discouraged.	−
Attribute 3: Strategic clarity	
Local committees are sufficiently aware of the party's strategy and goals.	+
Local committees do not understand what contribution is expected from them.	−
In this party, goals are not clearly defined.	−
Attribute 4: Organizational focus	
This party does not allow itself to get sidetracked by issues that do not really matter.	+
Few of the activities in this party center around things that are really vital to its success.	−
This party concentrates on activities that are fundamental to the success of the organization.	+
Attribute 5: Horizontal integration	
The sharing of information among local party organizations is not encouraged.	−
Local party committees are not encouraged to work together effectively toward the achievement of the party's goals.	−
The state party goes out of its way to ensure that different local party organizations cooperate in a coordinated way.	+

Attribute 6: Reward orientation

In this party, members are expected to contribute towards the achievement
of the party's objectives, and this is what is rewarded.   +

This party rewards those who contribute to the success of the organization
rather than those who have good connections.   +

In this party, there is not a clear link between reward and performance.   −

Attribute 7: Identification with the organization

Party members are personally committed to making the organization successful.   +

Party members do not experience a sense of belonging to this party.   −

Party members lack an emotional connection to the party.   −

Note: Signs indicate the valence of the item relative to the attribute scores and indexes; negative items were reverse coded.

parameters are inferred. Theoretically, there should be no variation across local chairs in their responses describing state organizational culture. To the extent variation occurs, it reflects different perceptions about the same thing. The survey asks respondents to *report* about party culture, and though some may have different perceptions about that culture, the culture itself does not vary across respondents. Rather than asking a group of respondents what their favorite color is, and then making an inference about this preference in a larger population, this reporting is much more like asking a group to say what color a particular object is. Some may say blue and some may say green—there may be measurement error—but the object has the same color. The accuracy of this reporting is evaluated not by assessing how well the mean and variation of a sample can be inferred to a population but by measuring how much agreement there is among the raters. As a result, sampling and statistical inference is not the appropriate tool to evaluate the validity of the culture measures. Instead, the culture responses need to be assessed in the context of *interrater agreement*. High interrater agreement suggests the existence of a coherent culture that is discernable among the respondents. Moreover, high interrater agreement in general provides greater confidence in the ratings for states in which the number of raters is small.

To measure interrater agreement, we utilize the $r_{WG(J)}$ statistic (James, Demaree, and Wolf 1984; LeBreton, James, and Lindell 2005). This statistic essentially captures the proportional reduction in error variance comparing the raters' agreement to random ratings. It is appropriate when there are multiple indicators. It is defined as follows:

$$r_{WG(J)} = \frac{J\left(1 - \dfrac{\overline{S}^2_{x_i}}{\sigma^2_{EU}}\right)}{J\left(1 - \dfrac{\overline{S}^2_{x_i}}{\sigma^2_{EU}}\right) + \left(\dfrac{\overline{S}^2_{x_i}}{\sigma^2_{EU}}\right)}$$

Where:
$\overline{S}^2_{x_i}$ = mean of observed variance for J indicators
σ^2_{EU} = $(A^2 - 1)/12$ = the expected variance resulting from random rating (i.e., equal probability of rating in each category), where A = the number of categories in an indicator

Table A.3 presents the average $r_{WG(J)}$ values on the seven attributes. The data are reported overall for the 83 state parties that had more than one rater and separately for the 43 Democratic parties and 40 Republican parties.[1] Generally, the scores support the validity of the measures. On average, $r_{WG(J)}$ values were above .70, which is often used as a rule of thumb.[2] There is, of course, variation across the parties in these values, but in the main the ratings seem to suggest that the local party chairs in most states have a high level of agreement in rating the culture of their party. The exception appears to be Horizontal Integration among the Democrats. Here,

TABLE A.3. Average Interrater Agreement Scores for Cultural Attributes across Parties

	Overall Average	Democratic Average	Republican Average
Culture management	.759	.758	.761
Innovativeness	.886	.970	.794
Strategic clarity	.776	.865	.678
Organizational focus	.840	.891	.784
Horizontal integration	.604	.491	.729
Reward orientation	.781	.802	.757
Identification with organization	.756	.708	.808

Note: Figures are average values of the $r_{WG(J)}$ statistic across the party organizations in the sample.

the raters' disagreement was substantial enough that doubts might be raised about whether a cultural norm or trait can be said to exist. Therefore, some caution must be exercised in analyzing this cultural facet. Overall, though, the measure appears valid. Given that the interrater agreement is high for states with many raters, we feel confident that the results from states with few raters are an accurate rating of the culture of those states.

Survey Instrument

Please answer the following questions to the best of your ability. Your responses are extremely important for understanding party organizations.

We greatly appreciate your cooperation.
Thank you,

Douglas D. Roscoe
Associate Professor of Political Science

Shannon Jenkins
Assistant Professor of Political Science

First, a few basic questions about your local party organization. Please select all of the items that describe your party organization.

( ) has a complete set of officers
( ) maintains a year round office
( ) has its own telephone listing
( ) has a website
( ) has email address(es)
( ) has social media account(s) (FaceBook, Twitter, etc.)
( ) has paid, full-time staff
( ) has a regular annual budget
( ) has paid, part-time staff
( ) operates headquarters during campaign season
( ) has a constitution, charter, or formal set of rules

In which of the following activities did your party organization engage in the 2008 election campaign?

( ) organized door to door canvassing
( ) organized campaign events (rallies, parades, etc.)
( ) arranged fund raising events
( ) conducted party fund raising online
( ) assisted a candidate with online fundraising
( ) sent mailings to voters
( ) distributed campaign literature
( ) organized telephone campaigns
( ) purchased billboard space
( ) distributed posters or lawn signs
( ) contributed money to candidates
( ) coordinated county level campaigns
( ) conducted registration drives
( ) utilized public opinion surveys
( ) publicized party and candidates through press releases
( ) publicized party and candidates through newspaper advertising
( ) publicized party and candidates by buying radio/TV time
( ) publicized party and candidates through email
( ) publicized party and candidates through a party website
( ) publicized party and candidates through social media (FaceBook, Twitter, etc.)
( ) coordinated local PAC activity
( ) conducted get-out-the-vote efforts

Does your local organization participate in any of the following activities with the state party organization?

( ) shares mailing lists of contributors and members
( ) joint fundraising programs
( ) cooperates in recruiting or checking on patronage appointments
( ) joint get-out-the-vote drives
( ) joint registration drives
( ) assists in identifying races targeted for extra funding and campaign efforts

Which of the following do you receive from the state party organization?

( ) assistance with financial record keeping
( ) legal advice
( ) computer services
( ) assistance with candidate recruitment

( ) funds for operating expenses
( ) funds for campaign expenses
( ) research
( ) office space
( ) staff
( ) campaign training and schools
( ) assistance with website development
( ) assistance with social media (FaceBook, Twitter, etc.)

Next, we have some questions about your views on your party as a whole in your state. For the following questions, the term "party" is used to refer to all of the party committees (state and local) that constitute your party organization. Please click on the best response.

Strongly Agree	**Agree**	**Neutral**	**Disagree**	**Strongly Disagree**
In this party, members are expected to contribute towards the achievement of the party's objectives, and this is what is rewarded.				
Party members are personally committed to making the organization successful.				
Decisions about party policy are made by state leadership with little input from local committees.				
The sharing of information among local party organizations is not encouraged.				
This party does not allow itself to get side-tracked by issues that do not really matter.				
Local committees are sufficiently aware of the party's strategy and goals.				
This party has strong values which are widely shared by its members.				
Ideas tend to percolate up from the local committees and rarely come down from the state party leadership.				
This party believes that achieving individual local committee goals is more important than collective party goals.				
Electoral viability is valued more than ideological agreement in a party candidate.				
Local party committees are not encouraged to work together effectively toward the achievement of the party's goals.				
Local committees do not understand what contribution is expected from them.				
Party members are given wide latitude in accomplishing goals without much direction from state leadership.				
The party rarely holds events designed to create a shared sense of direction and accomplishment.				
Local parties are encouraged to be creative and innovative.				

Strongly Agree	**Agree**	**Neutral**	**Disagree**	**Strongly Disagree**

This party rewards those who contribute to the success of the organization rather than those who have good connections.

The party believes it is more important to act quickly to achieve party goals than to use established decision making procedures.

The party emphasizes the importance of exploring and discussing all options when making decisions more than making decisions quickly and efficiently.

Few of the activities in this party center around things that are really vital to its success.

The state party goes out of its way to ensure that different local party organizations cooperate in a coordinated way.

Candidates who agree with party positions get more support than candidates who are most likely to win.

This party concentrates on activities that are fundamental to the success of the organization.

When this party makes decisions, getting things done efficiently is more valued than ensuring consensus.

Local parties are always encouraged to be flexible to changes in the external environment.

Information is disseminated down from the state committee and rarely flows up from local committees or laterally among local committees.

This party values following the rules to reach decisions in the right way more than making decisions quickly.

This is not an innovative organization and new ideas about winning elections are generally discouraged.

Power in this party flows from the bottom up, rather than from the top down.

Party members do not experience a sense of belonging to this party.

Party members lack a clear understanding of what its values and philosophies are.

Getting state committee work accomplished usually comes before local committee work.

In this party, goals are not clearly defined.

Party members lack an emotional connection to the party.

In this party, there is not a clear link between reward and performance.

When doing party work, members are given explicit instructions and are obligated to follow rules and regulations.

What is your age? _______ years old.

What is your gender? ( ) Male ( ) Female

What is your racial background? _________________________

Please indicate the highest level of formal education you have completed.
( ) grade school   ( ) some college
( ) high school   ( ) undergraduate degree

Below is a scale on which the political views people might hold are listed. Where would you place yourself on this scale? Please indicate the term that best describes you.
( ) very liberal
( ) liberal
( ) somewhat liberal
( ) moderate, middle of the road
( ) somewhat conservative
( ) conservative
( ) very conservative

THANK YOU VERY MUCH FOR YOUR TIME AND COOPERATION!

If you would like to provide additional comments, please do so below.

____

____

____

____

____

____

____

Notes

Chapter 1. Party Organizations in Their Environment

1. It is interesting to note that the new role Kellor desired for parties—their "expansion elsewhere"—was essentially the one fulfilled by think tanks in the 20th century. She advocated for parties to be involved in "social research" and to act as "a general clearing-house for information." Parties could become the location of a "political laboratory" to "cover the whole range of social and economic life" (Kellor 1914, 883). To be sure, there was a need for this kind of activity in the dawning era of social science. Indeed, arguably the first American think tank, the Brookings Institution, was founded in 1916, only two years after Kellor wrote. It is a testament to the enduring attractiveness of parties' electoral capabilities that parties remained focused on elections, and other organizations emerged to take on this new social research function.

2. Whether organizational change is similar to or actually is a process of evolution can be a matter of debate. Organizations, as we discuss later, have an intentionality and a diversity of goals that differentiate them from most (though not all) biological entities. A resolution of this question is not necessary for our purposes here, because the utility of evolution theory for understanding organizational change remains the same under either perspective.

3. This is the key, but not the only, source of biological selection. In recent years, studies have uncovered evidence that the environment of the parent can shape the characteristics of the offspring. These effects are considered epigenetic, because they result not from changes to the DNA but to the mechanisms surrounding the way genetic code is translated into physical traits. The variation in traits resulting from these inherited epigenetic factors can, of course, correspond to differences in survival and reproduction and so can be a source of natural selection.

4. The difficulty of altering the routines and structures of restaurants is highlighted by Chef Gordon Ramsay's television program, *Kitchen Nightmares*. Faced with dwindling numbers of customers and moribund revenues, restaurant owners still find it difficult to change the fundamentals of their business. They call in Ramsay, who with monumental effort, and appropriate television drama, attempts to remake the restaurant's concept and practices. Despite the fact that all appears

well at the end of each episode (as befits compelling reality TV), follow-ups reiterate the difficult nature of organizational change; less than 10% of restaurants featured in the first two seasons are still open, although success rates have increased since then (Ryland 2013).

5. Holbrook and La Raja (2013) report that automatic retention of ballot access across the states requires a party to get somewhere between 0.5% to 20% in the previous election, with a median of 2%. In three states, parties can remain on the ballot indefinitely. While third parties may occasionally reach these thresholds, they have difficulty maintaining them, given the electoral rules establishing first-past-the-post, winner-take-all, single-member district processes. Democrats and Republicans easily meet these thresholds on a consistent basis, eliminating any concern about ballot access.

6. Perhaps the best example of a business firm with such governmental protection was AT&T and its subsidiaries, Western Electric and Bell Labs. As Gertner (2012) shows, this protection was a key ingredient in the success of Bell Labs, helping to sustain its unique culture and foster its impressive record of innovation. The record of AT&T and Bell Labs underscores one of the points we make in this chapter—protection need not hamper innovation and adaptation and may, in some cases, catalyze it.

7. Koger, Masket, and Noel (2009) make a good case that the team view is not even adequate for the broader concept of *party*. In their view, the party is really an extended network of actors, including interest groups and media outlets.

Chapter 2. Connections and Cooperation in the State Party Confederacy

1. See http://www.thedailyshow.com/watch/wed-october-23-2013/suppressing-the-vote.

2. See http://massdems.org/state-committee/governance/charter/article-two/.

3. See the appendix for a full description of the survey, including the survey instrument and response rates.

4. For stylistic reasons, we have reordered the factors in this discussion and in table 2.1 compared to the order of the actual loadings in the factor matrix. In actuality, Special Assistance was factor 1 (eigenvalue = 1.978), Internet Assistance was factor 2 (eigenvalue = 0.554), Expenses Assistance was factor 3 (eigenvalue = 0.349), and Core Assistance was factor 4 (eigenvalue = 0.140). These eigenvalues do suggest the dominance of special assistance as the main dimension of state assistance. In terms of model selection, all of these eigenvalues fall near or above the mean eigenvalue (0.171), and, as mentioned already, the AIC and BIC statistics both suggest a four-factor model is optimal.

5. Analysis of the standard deviation in state party assistance includes only those states where 10 or more counties responded to the survey. See the appendix for response rates.

6. Bernstein, Bromley, and Meyer (2006) examine the party culture of Democrats and Republicans by looking at differences in preferences on political heroes, television shows, magazines, and music rather than the operation of party organizations. Nonetheless, they find clear differences between Democrats and Republicans on these measures, supporting the idea that there are distinct cultures in the two major US parties.

7. The appendix has a fuller discussion of the measurement of organizational culture at the state level, including an analysis of interrater agreement among survey respondents.

8. In the discussion in this section only states with more than one respondent are included. In the analyses in chapter 3, we include all states, even with single raters. As we discuss in the appendix, the measurement of state party culture is a ratings process, not a sampling process, so small Ns are not a problem as long as the interrater agreement is generally high. The average interrater agreement across all attributes was .772, with a low of .604 for Horizontal Integration and a high of .886 for Innovativeness. Moreover, our analysis shows that the number of respondents was not significantly related to measures of interrater agreement. In other words, raters have high levels of agreement, so only a few raters can provide an accurate picture.

9. The BIC value suggests a two-factor model, but the eigenvalues drop sharply after the first factor. For example, the first factor encompasses over 97% of the variation, and the second factor's eigenvalue falls below the mean eigenvalue. The second factor, to the extent it exists, is very weak.

Chapter 3. Organizational Structure and Activity at the Local Level

1. While the PTS and the EDP both examined levels of party structure and activity in the past, an examination of how *individual* party organizations adapt over time is not possible for several reasons. First, the PTS data, which rely on a sample of all party organizations in the United States, only exist in aggregate form at this point in time. Second, the EDP relies on a sample of eight to nine states to report party structure and activity. So while these data do still exist for individual local party committees, the overlap between the EDP and this survey is small, making over time comparisons unreliable. As our focus here is on the adaptation of individual organizations to the environment, we are relying on a cross-section of individual organizations and summarize here analysis of aggregate changes in local party structure and activity; see Roscoe and Jenkins (2014) for a more detailed analysis of these aggregate changes.

2. To be sure, local party committees also reflect the national political environment, but there are several reasons why we cannot and do not test that effect here. First, these local party committees reside in the same national political environment. To understand the effect of national environmental variation would require data on local party organizations in different countries or over time in the

United States, something that is beyond the scope of our data here. Of course, we do examine partisan differences, which gets at how national Democrats and Republicans approach working with local parties differently, so we can and we do speak to those differences here. Moreover, national party assistance to local parties generally speaking flows through state political parties, so we think it is more appropriate to examine top-down influence through the lens of the state political party.

3. There is some logic behind an alternative hypothesis suggesting greater structure and activity as party *dominance*, not competition, increases—in other words, one might expect parties with the most local support to also have the most resources available and thus to be most mature and active. Interestingly, the data do not support this hypothesis, even at a rudimentary level. First, the bivariate relationship is opposite for Democrats and Republicans. More dominant (as measured by the local share of the party's average presidential vote in 2004 and 2008) Democratic parties are more structurally mature and more active, but more dominant Republican committees are less mature and active, though the relationships are not large. But, in the multivariate models, these relationships completely disappear. For these reasons, we use the folded competition variable in the models.

4. The basic unit of analysis in these models is the local party committee. In most cases, this committee is associated with a county. However, in some states (CT, MA, RI, and VA), some or all of the local committees are town based. And in other states (AK, ND) the committees coincide with state legislative districts. As a result, electoral data come from several sources. The county-level presidential data come from *Congressional Quarterly* via the Census Bureau's data interface. Data for Massachusetts towns come from the *Boston Globe* website for 2008 and the state's official Election Statistics book (PD 43) for 2004, and the remaining data for Alaska, Connecticut, North Dakota, Rhode Island, and Virginia come from their official state websites.

5. Urbanization rates at the local level were not available for the 2010 census at the time the datasets were compiled.

Chapter 4. The Electoral Payoff

1. See http://uselectionatlas.org/.

2. Here and throughout this chapter, we use simple slopes to more easily convey the effects for Democrats and Republicans. Because party is coded 0 for Democrats and 1 for Republicans, the simple slope for Democrats is the coefficient for the activity variable and the simple slope for the Republicans is the sum of that coefficient and the interaction term. Standard errors have been reconstituted from the variance-covariance matrix. For more on simple slopes, see Preacher, Curran, and Bauer 2006.

3. It is important to note that the competitive context variable is entered into the model the same way for Democrats and Republicans. For example, for both a local Republican party and a local Democratic party in Alabama, the variable

takes the value of −1. The interaction term with party allows the context to have opposing effects for the different parties. In subsequent examinations of the regression models, the favorable/competitive/unfavorable labels are applied accordingly (e.g., a local Republican party in Alabama is in a favorable context, the Democrats in an unfavorable one).

4. This is not only partly a result of sampling but also a population-level phenomenon reflecting the differing number of local units in blue versus red states.

Chapter 5. The Future of Local Party Organizations

1. There is a misconception that Tea Party supporters tend to be more libertarian than conservative Republicans. However, Arceneaux and Nicholson (2012) demonstrate that Tea Partiers are very conservative on social issues, falling in line with traditional conservative views. Moreover, racial animus is not a particularly strong dimension of their belief systems—no more so than other conservatives.

2. Interestingly, results from primaries in 2014 suggest the Republicans are adapting to these challenges, as establishment candidates have pushed back Tea Party primary challengers.

3. Haidt (2012) argues effectively that the evolution of humans occurred in part at a group level, and that the characteristic he calls "groupishness" granted advantages that have led to its selection and retention among humans today. Haidt makes the case that the nature of our group affiliations are expressed in a number of moral matrices and that, to a significant extent, liberals and conservatives in the United States today cluster around different combinations of these matrices. From this perspective, then, contemporary tribes in American politics are deeply embedded in our psychology and biology.

4. Some political organizations and interest groups, recognizing this fact, have attempted to make forays into building local organizations on the ground. For example, MoveOn has Local Councils to push the organization's agenda—with very modest success. A search of the MoveOn Council website for the zip code of our home institution reveals one council within a 30-mile radius, and that one is a council for an entire state. The National Organization for Women is another example, as research has shown that NOW local chapters, such as they still exist, typically struggle to survive (Reger and Staggenborg 2006). Lacking legal protection, groups have found it hard to build and maintain local organizations.

5. One caveat to this conclusion about partisan identification, often ignored in the media, is the surprising variation in the partisan leanings of Tea Party supporters. In the 2012 ANES, just under 13% say they lean toward the Democratic Party or are outright Democratic identifiers, and almost 7% of that 13% call themselves strong Democrats. Of course, this is much smaller than the overall population, but the data do suggest caution in conclusions about the Tea Party's position as the right wing of the Republican Party. Pertinent to the analysis here, though, is the fact that when Tea Partiers do identify with the Democrats, they are more likely to be

strong partisans than to be weak partisans or leaners; in the population overall, the opposite is true. So, even when claiming a Democratic identification, Tea Partiers tend to have an unusually strong tribal affiliation.

6. Actually, all of the campaign committees regulated by the FEC are technically 527 organizations, but their decision to engage in express electoral activity triggers an additional classification that requires reporting to the FEC. For example, PACs, parties, and candidate committees that accept or contribute campaign funds are all 527 organizations that are subject to FEC rules and reporting requirements. Similarly, a 527 that does engage in express advocacy is classified as an Independent Expenditure Only Committee, or Super PAC, and must report to the FEC (we discuss Super PACs later in the chapter). In practice, the term "527" is used only for those 527 organizations that limit their activity to issue advocacy.

7. The electioneering communication provisions held during the 60 days prior to a general election and 30 days prior to a primary election. The ads also had to be "targeted," which essentially meant they were directed toward an election constituency. This provision of the law was meant to remove the wink-and-nod approach to express advocacy. However, the Supreme Court, in *Wisconsin Right to Life v. FEC* (2007) and later in *Citizens United v. FEC* (2010), concluded that it failed to give wide enough berth to non-electoral speech and struck it down.

8. Moreover, a federal court has ruled that a single 527 can collect both regular PAC money to use for regulated contributions to candidates and also collect unregulated money for independent expenditures (provided the funds are segregated).

9. These party-centered Super PACs, and the amount they spent, are: American Crossroads ($104.7 million), Majority PAC ($38.1 million), House Majority PAC ($30.7 million), Congressional Leadership Fund ($9.5 million), Young Guns Action Fund ($4.7 million), End the Gridlock ($1.7 million), New Prosperity Foundation ($1.6 million), Super PAC for America ($1.4 million), and National Horizon ($1.2 million) (Magleby 2014).

10. The FEC does not specifically identify local parties in its datasets, so a coding decision needed to be made to build figure 5.3. If the title of a party committee contained "county," "town," "district"; an abbreviated form of those; or contained the actual name of a local community/region, it was designated as local. Excluded from the local definitions were organizations with "club" in the title.

Appendix. Local Party Chair Survey

1. Only three state parties, all Democratic, had only one respondent.

2. There have been criticisms of this rule of thumb (Harvey and Hollander 2004). One alternative is to assess whether the level of agreement is different enough from random ratings to be statistically significant. However, this can only indicate that some agreement exists beyond chance, not whether it is adequate agreement. At the very least, one must take caution using ratings with scores well below .70.

References

Abramowitz, Alan I. 2011. "Partisan Polarization and the Rise of the Tea Party Movement." Paper Presented at the 2011 Annual Meeting of the American Political Science Association, Seattle, WA.

Aldrich, Howard E. 1979. *Organizations and Environments.* Englewood Cliffs, NJ: Prentice Hall.

Aldrich, John H. 2000. "Southern Parties in State and Nation." *Journal of Politics* 62(3): 643–670.

Appleton, Andrew W., and Daniel S. Ward. 1997. "Party Response to Environmental Change: A Model of Organizational Innovation." *Party Politics* 3(3): 341–362.

APSACPP. 1950. "Toward a More Responsible Two-Party System: A Report of the Committee on Political Parties." *American Political Science Review* 44(3): Supplement, Part 2.

Arceneaux, Kevin, and Stephen P. Nicholson. 2012. "Who Wants to Have a Tea Party? The Who, What, and Why of the Tea Party Movement." *PS* (October): 700–710.

Beck, Paul, and Erik Heidemann. 2014. "Changing Strategies in Grassroots Canvassing: 1956–2012." *Party Politics* 20(2): 261–274.

Bergan, Daniel E., Alan S. Gerber, Donald P. Green, and Costas Panagopoulos. 2005. "Grassroots Mobilization and Voter Turnout in 2004." *Public Opinion Quarterly* 69: 760–77.

Bernstein, Jonathan, Rebecca E. Bromley, and Krystle T. Meyer. 2006. "Republicans and Golf, Democrats and Outkast: Or, Party Political Culture from the Top Down." *The Forum* 4, Article 8.

Bibby, John F. 2002. "State Party Organizations: Strengthened and Adapting to Candidate-Centered Politics and Nationalization." In *The Parties Respond: Changes in American Parties and Campaigns,* 4th ed., ed. L. Sandy Maisel. Boulder, CO: Westview, 19–46.

Bibby, John F., and Thomas Holbrook. 1996. "Parties and Elections." In *Politics in the American States: A Comparative Analysis,* 6th ed., ed. Virginia Gray and Herbert Jacobs. Washington, DC: CQ Press, 78–121.

Bickhard, Mark H., and Donald T. Campbell. 2003. "Variations in Variation and Selection: The Ubiquity of the Variation-and-Selective-Retention Ratchet in Emergent Organizational Complexity." *Foundations of Science* 8(3): 215–282.

Brady, Henry E., Sidney Verba, and Kay Lehman Schlozman. 1995. "Beyond SES: A Resource Model of Political Participation." *American Political Science Review* 89(June): 271–294.

Brock, Martha. 2011. "Are the Political Parties Irrelevant in the Age of Social Media?" www.examiner.com. http://www.examiner.com/article/are-the-political-parties-now-irrelevant-the-age-of-social-media. Accessed 16 April 2014.

Broder, David S. 1972a. *The Party's Over: The Failure of Politics in America*. New York: Harper Colophon.

Broder, David S. 1972b. "The Party's Over." *The Atlantic Monthly* 229(3): 33–39.

Cameron, Kim S., and Robert E. Quinn. 1999. *Diagnosing and Changing Organizational Culture*. Upper Saddle River, NJ: Prentice-Hall.

Campbell, Donald T. 1965. "Variation and Selective Retention in Socio-Cultural Evolution." In *Social Change in Developing Areas: A Reinterpretation of Evolutionary Theory*, ed. Herbert R. Barringer, George I. Blanksten, and Raymond W. Mack. Cambridge, MA: Schenkman, 19–49.

Carroll, Glen R. 1984. "Organizational Ecology." *Annual Review of Sociology* 10: 71–93.

Chatman, Jennifer A. 1989. "Improving Interactional Organizational Research: A Model of Person-Organization Fit." *The Academy of Management Review* 14: 333–349.

Chatman, Jennifer A. 1991. "Matching People and Organizations: Selection and Socialization in Public Accounting Firms." *Administrative Science Quarterly* 36: 459–484.

Clark, Peter B., and James Q. Wilson. 1961. "Incentive Systems: A Theory of Organizations." *Administrative Science Quarterly* 6(2): 129–166.

Clarke, Phillipa J., and Blair Wheaton. 2007. "Addressing Data Sparseness in Contextual Population Research: Using Cluster Analysis to Create Synthetic Neighborhoods." *Sociological Methods and Research* 35(3): 311–351.

Conway, M. Margaret, and Frank B. Feigert. 1968. "Motivation, Incentive Systems, and the Political Party Organization." *American Political Science Review* 62(4): 1159–1173.

Cotter, Cornelius P., James L. Gibson, John F. Bibby, and Robert J. Huckshorn. 1984. *Party Organizations in American Politics*. New York: Praeger.

Cziko, Gary. 1995. *Without Miracles: Universal Selection Theory and the Second Darwinian Revolution*. Cambridge, MA: MIT Press.

Dawkins, Richard. 1983. "Universal Darwinism." In *Evolution from Molecules to Man*, ed. D. S. Bendall. Cambridge: Cambridge University Press, 403–425.

Denison, Daniel R. 1990. *Corporate Culture and Organizational Effectiveness*. New York, NY: Wiley.

Denison, Daniel R. 1996. "What Is the Difference between Organizational Culture and Organizational Climate? A Native's Point of View on a Decade of Paradigm Wars." *Academy of Management Journal* 21: 619–654.

Democratic National Committee (DNC). 2014. "The 50-State Strategy." http://www.democrats.org/about/fifty_state_strategy. Accessed 30 May 2014.

Downs, Anthony. 1957. *An Economic Theory of Democracy*. New York, NY: Harper.

Dwyre, Diana, Eric Heberlig, Robin Kolodny, and Bruce Larson. 2007. "Committees and Candidates: National Party Finance after BCRA." In *The State of the Parties: The Changing Role of Contemporary American Parties*, 5th ed., ed. John C. Green and Daniel J. Coffey. New York, NY: Rowman & Littlefield, 95–112.

Eldersveld, Samuel J. 1964. *Political Parties: A Behavioral Analysis*. Chicago, IL: Rand McNally.

Epstein, Leon D. 1986. *Political Parties in the American Mold*. Madison, WI: University of Wisconsin Press.

Farnsworth, Stephen J., and Diana Owen. 2004. "Internet Use and the 2000 Presidential Election." *Electoral Studies* 23: 415–429.

Fox News. 2009. "Thousands of Anti-Tax 'Tea Party' Protestors Turn Out in US Cities." foxnews.com. April 15. http://www.foxnews.com/politics/2009/04/15/thousands-anti-tax-tea-party-protesters-turn-cities/#.

Francia, Peter L., and Jonathan S. Morris. 2014. "Divided Republicans? Tea Party Supporters, Establishment Republicans, and Social Networks." In *State of the Parties: The Changing Role of Contemporary American Parties*, 7th ed., ed. John C. Green, Daniel Coffey, and David Cohen. Lanham, MD: Rowman & Littlefield, 175–190.

Freeman, Jo. 1986. "The Political Culture of the Democratic and Republican Parties." *Political Science Quarterly* 101: 327–356.

Frendreis, John P., and Alan R. Gitelson. 1993. "Local Parties in an Age of Change." American Review of Politics 14: 533–547.

Frendreis, John P., and Alan R. Gitelson. 1999. "Local Parties in the 1990s: Spokes in a Candidate-Centered Wheel." In *The State of the Parties: The Changing Role of Contemporary American Parties*, 3rd ed., ed. John C. Green and Daniel M. Shea. Lanham, MD: Rowman & Littlefield, 135–153.

Frendreis, John P., James L. Gibson, and Laura L. Vertz. 1990. "The Electoral Relevance of Local Party Organizations." *American Political Science Review* 84(1): 225–235.

Gerber, Alan S., and Donald P. Green. 2000. "The Effects of Canvassing, Telephone Calls, and Direct Mail on Voter Turnout: A Field Experiment." *American Political Science Review* 94: 653–663.

Gertner, Jon. 2012. *The Idea Factory: Bell Labs and the Great Age of American Innovation*. New York, NY: Penguin Press.

Gibson, James, John Ivancevich Jr., James Donnelly, and Robert Konopaske. 2002. *Organizations: Behavior, Structure, Processes*, 11th ed. New York, NY: McGraw Hill.

Gibson, James L., Cornelius O. Cotter, John F. Bibby, and Robert J. Huckshorn. 1983. "Assessing Party Organizational Strength." *American Journal of Political Science* 27: 193–222.

Gibson, James L., Cornelius P. Cotter, John F. Bibby, and Robert J. Huckshorn. 1985. "Whither the Local Parties? A Cross-Sectional and Longitudinal

Analysis of the Strength of Party Organization." *American Journal of Political Science* 29(February): 139–160.

Gibson, James. L., John P. Frendreis, and Laura L. Vertz. 1989. "Party Dynamics in the 1980s: Change in County Party Organizational Strength, 1980–1984." *American Journal of Political Science* 33(February): 67–90.

Goldstein, Harvey. 2011. *Multilevel Statistical Models*, 4th ed. New York, NY: Wiley.

Green, Donald, Bradley Palmquist, and Eric Schickler. 2002. *Partisan Hearts and Minds: Political Parties and the Social Identities of Voters*. New Haven, CT: Yale University Press.

Greene, Steven. 2004. "Social Identity Theory and Party Identification." *Social Science Quarterly* 85(1): 136–153.

Gregory, K. L. 1983. "Native-View Paradigms: Multiple Cultures and Culture Conflicts in Organizations." *Administrative Science Quarterly* 28(3): 359–376.

Haidt, Jonathan. 2012. *The Righteous Mind: Why Good People Are Divided by Politics and Religion*. New York, NY: Pantheon.

Hamby, Peter. 2013. "First on CNN: Republicans Launch Their Own '50-State Strategy.'" http://politicalticker.blogs.cnn.com/2013/07/24/first-on-cnn-republicans-launch-their-own-50-state-strategy/. Accessed 1 May 2014.

Hannan, Michael T., and John Freeman. 1989. *Organizational Ecology*. Cambridge, MA: Harvard University Press.

Harvey, Robert J., and Eran Hollander. 2004. "Benchmarking r_{WG} Interrater Agreement Indices: Let's Drop the .70 Rule-of-Thumb." Paper presented at the Annual Conference of the Society for Industrial and Organizational Psychology, Chicago.

Herrnson, Paul S. 2002. "National Party Organizations at the Dawn of the Twenty-First Century." In *The Parties Respond: Changes in American Parties and Campaigns*, 4th ed., ed. L. Sandy Maisel. Boulder, CO: Westview, 47–78.

Hodgson, Geoffrey M. 2005. "Generalizing Darwinism to Social Evolution: Some Early Attempts." *Journal of Economic Issues* 39(4): 899–914.

Hofstede, Geert, Bram Neuijen, Denise Daval Ohayv, and Geert Sanders. 1990. "Measuring Organizational Cultures: A Qualitative and Quantitative Study across Twenty Cases." *Administrative Science Quarterly* 35(2): 286–316.

Hogan, Robert E. 2002. "Candidate Perceptions of Political Party Campaign Activity in State Legislative Elections." *State Politics and Policy Quarterly* 2: 66–85.

Holbrook, Thomas M., and Raymond L. La Raja. 2008. "Parties and Elections." In *Politics in the American States: A Comparative Analysis*, 9th ed., ed. Virginia Gray and Russell L. Hanson. Washington, DC: CQ Press, 61–97.

Holbrook, Thomas M., and Raymond L. La Raja. 2013. "Parties and Elections." In *Politics in the American States: A Comparative Analysis*, 10th ed., ed. Virginia Gray, Russell L. Hanson, and Thad Kousser. Washington, DC: Sage/CQ Press, 63–104.

Hox, Joop. 1998. "Multilevel Modeling: When and Why?" In *Classification, Data Analysis, and Data Highways*, ed. I. Balderjahn, R. Mathar, and M. Schader. New York: Springer Verlag, 147–154.

James, Lawrence R., Robert G. Demaree, and Gerrit Wolf. 1984. "Estimating Within-Group Interrater Reliability with and without Response Bias." *Journal of Applied Psychology* 69: 85–98.

Jenkins, Shannon, and Douglas D. Roscoe. 2011. "State Party Integration." Paper Presented at the 2011 State Politics and Policy Annual Conference in Hanover, NH.

Keith, Bruce E., David B. Magleby, Candice J. Nelson, Elizabeth Orr, Mark C. Westlye, and Raymond E. Wolfinger. 1992. *The Myth of the Independent Voter.* Berkeley, CA: University of California Press.

Kellor, Frances A. 1914. "A New Spirit in Party Organization." *North American Review* 199 (June): 879–892.

Key, V. O., Jr. 1958. *Politics, Parties, and Pressure Groups,* 3rd ed. New York, NY: Crowell.

Koger, Gregory, Seth Masket, and Hans Noel. 2009. "Partisan Webs: Information Exchange and Party Networks." *British Journal of Political Science* 39: 633–653.

Kovacs, Joe. 2013. "Rush Limbaugh Explodes on Republican Party." www.wnd.com. http://www.wnd.com/2013/10/rush-explodes-on-irrelevant-republicans/. Accessed 16 April 2014.

La Raja, Raymond J. 2003. "State Parties and Soft Money: How Much Party Building?" In *The State of the Parties: The Changing Role of Contemporary American Parties,* 4th ed., ed. John C. Green and Rick Farmer New York, NY: Rowman & Littlefield, 132–150.

La Raja, Raymond J., Susan E. Orr, and Daniel Smith. 2006. "Surviving BCRA: State Party Finance in 2004." In *State of the Parties: The Changing Role of Contemporary American Parties,* 5th ed., ed. John C. Green and Daniel Coffey. New York: Rowman & Littlefield, 113–134.

LeBreton, James M., Lawrence R. James, and Michael K. Lindell. 2005. "Recent Issues Regarding r_{WG}, r^*_{WG}, $r_{WG(J)}$, and $R^*_{WG(J)}$." *Organizational Research Methods* 8: 128–138.

Levendusky, Matthew. 2009. *The Partisan Sort: How Liberals Became Democrats and Conservatives Became Republicans.* Chicago, IL: University of Chicago Press.

Lewis, Orion A., and Sven Steinmo. 2012. "How Institutions Evolve: Evolutionary Theory and Institutional Change." *Polity* 44(3): 314–339.

Lowery, David, and Virginia Gray. 1995. "The Population Ecology of Gucci Gulch, or the Natural Regulation of Interest Group Numbers in the American States." *American Journal of Political Science* 39(1): 1–29.

Lowery, David, and Virginia Gray. 2000. *The Population Ecology of Interest Representation.* Ann Arbor, MI: University of Michigan Press.

Luthans, Fred. 1995. *Organizational Behavior,* 7th ed. New York: McGraw-Hill.

Magleby, David B. 2014. "Towards a Typology of Super PACs: Candidate, Party, or Group Centered?" In *State of the Parties: The Changing Role of Contemporary American Parties,* 7th ed., ed. John C. Green, Daniel Coffey, and David Cohen. Lanham, MD: Rowman & Littlefield, 231–250.

McCarty, Nolan M., Keith T. Poole, and Howard Rosenthal. 2006. *Polarized America: The Dance of Ideology and Unequal Riches*. Cambridge, MA: MIT Press.

Meyer, Marshall W. 1990. "Notes of a Skeptic: From Organizational Ecology to Organizational Evolution." In *Organizational Evolution: New Directions*, ed. Jitendra V. Singh. Newbury Park, CA: Sage, 298–314.

Nelson, Richard R. 2007. "Universal Darwinism and Evolutionary Social Science." *Biology and Philosophy* 22(1): 73–94.

Nelson, Richard R., and Sidney G. Winter. 1982. *An Evolutionary Theory of Economic Change*. Cambridge, MA: Harvard University Press.

Norrander, Barbara, and Jay Wendland. 2014. "State Primary Laws and the Ideological Composition of Primary Electorates." Paper presented at the 2014 Annual State Politics and Policy Conference, Bloomington, IN.

O'Reilly, Charles A., III, Jennifer Chatman, and David Caldwell. 1991. "People and Organizational Culture: A Profile-Comparison Approach to Assessing Person-Organization Fit." *The Academy of Management Journal* 34: 487–516.

Perrow, Charles. 1979. *Complex Organizations: A Critical Essay*, 2nd ed. Glenview, IL: Scott Foresman.

Post, W. Z. van der, T. J. de Coning, and E. vd M. Smit. 1997. "An Instrument to Measure Political Culture." *South African Journal of Business Management* 28: 148–168.

Preacher, Kristopher J., Patrick J. Curran, and Daniel J. Bauer. 2006. "Computational Tools for Probing Interactions in Multiple Linear Regression, Multilevel Modeling, and Latent Curve Analysis." *Journal of Educational and Behavioral Statistics* 31(Winter): 437–348.

Rapoport, Ronald, Meredith Dost, and Walter Stone. 2014. "The Tea Party, Republican Factionalism, and the 2012 Election." In *State of the Parties: The Changing Role of Contemporary American Parties*, 7th ed., ed. John C. Green, Daniel Coffey, and David Cohen. Lanham, MD: Rowman & Littlefield, 157–174.

Ravasi, Davide, and Majken Schultz. 2006. "Responding to Organizational Identity Threats: Exploring the Role of Organizational Culture." *Academy of Management Journal* 49(3): 433–458.

Reger, Jo, and Suzanne Staggenborg. 2006. "Patterns of Mobilization in Local Movement Organizations: Leadership and Strategy in Four National Organization for Women Chapters." *Sociological Perspectives* 49: 297–323.

Reich, Robert. 2014. "Political Parties Irrelevant in the Age of the Super PAC." www.sfgate.com. http://www.sfgate.com/opinion/reich/article/Political-parties-irrelevant-in-the-age-of-the-5377548.php. Accessed 16 April 2014.

Robbins, Liz. 2009. "Tax Day Is Met with Tea Parties." *New York Times*. April 15. http://www.nytimes.com/2009/04/16/us/politics/16taxday.html?_r=0.

Robbins, Stephen. 2005. *Essentials of Organizational Behavior*, 8th ed. Upper Saddle River, NJ: Prentice Hall.

Roscoe, Douglas D., and Neil D. Christiansen. 2010. "Exploring the Attitudinal Structure of Partisanship." *Journal of Applied Social Psychology* 40(9): 2232–2266.

Roscoe, Douglas D., and Shannon Jenkins. 2014. "Changes in Local Party Structure and Activity, 1980–2008." In *The State of the Parties: The Changing Role of Contemporary American Parties*, 7th ed., ed. John C. Green, Daniel J. Coffey, and David Cohen. Lanham, MD: Rowman & Littlefield, 287–302.

Rosenstone, Steven, and John M. Hansen. 1993. *Mobilization, Participation, and Democracy in America*. New York: Macmillan.

Rousseau, Denise M. 1990. "Quantitative Assessment of Organizational Culture: The Case for Multiple Measures." In *Frontiers in Industrial and Organizational Psychology*, vol. 3, ed. Benjamin Schneider. San Francisco, CA: Jossey-Bass, 303–322.

Ryland, Amber. 2013. "Kitchen Nightmares Fail! Gordon Ramsay Only Saved 2 of the 21 Restaurants in the First Two Seasons." http://radaronline.com/exclusives/2013/07/kitchen-nightmares-gordon-ramsay-fail-first-two-seasons/. Accessed 4 February 2014.

Sabato, Larry J., and Bruce Larson. 2002. *The Party's Just Begun: Shaping Political Parties for America's Future*, 2nd ed. New York, NY: Longman.

Salisbury, Robert H. 1969. "An Exchange Theory of Interest Groups." *Midwest Journal of Political Science* 13(1): 1–32.

Schaffner, Brian F. 2012. *Politics, Parties, and Elections in America*, 7th ed. Boston, MA: Wadsworth.

Schein, Edgar H. 1992. *Organizational Culture and Leadership*, 2nd ed. San Francisco, CA: Jossey-Bass.

Schlesinger, Joseph A. 1984. "On the Theory of Party Organization." *Journal of Politics* 46(2): 369–400.

Shea, Daniel M. 2014. "Separated We Stand? The Impact of Ideological Sorting on Local Party Dynamics." In *State of the Parties: The Changing Role of Contemporary American Parties*, 7th ed., ed. John C. Green, Daniel Coffey, and David Cohen. Lanham, MD: Rowman & Littlefield, 303–322.

Snijders, Tom, and Roel Bosker. 1999. *Multilevel Analysis: An Introduction to Basic and Advanced Multilevel Modeling*. Sage.

Somashekhar, Sandhya. 2010. "Tea Party Activists March on Capitol Hill." *Washington Post*. September 12. http://www.washingtonpost.com/wp-dyn/content/article/2010/09/12/AR2010091201425.html.

Stanley, Steven M. 1979. *Macroevolution: Pattern and Process*. San Francisco, CA: W. H. Freeman.

Tajfel, Henri, and John C. Turner. 1986. "The Social Identity Theory of Intergroup Behavior." In *Psychology of Intergroup Behavior*, ed. Stephen Worchel and William G. Austin. Chicago: Nelson-Hall, 7–24.

Trice, Harrison M., and Janice M. Beyer. 1993. *The Cultures of Work Organizations*. Englewood Cliffs, NJ: Prentice-Hall.

Turner, John C., and Henri Tajfel. 1979. "Social Comparison and Group Interest in Ingroup Favoritism." *European Journal of Social Psychology* 9(2): 187–204.

Williams, Andrew Paul, Kaye D. Trammell, Monica Postelnicu, Kristen D. Landreville, and Justin D. Martin. 2005. "Blogging and Hyperlinking: Use of the Web to Enhance Viability during the 2004 US Campaign." *Journalism Studies* 6: 177–186.

Williamson, Vanessa, Theda Skocpol, and John Coggin. 2011. "The Tea Party and the Remaking of Republican Conservatism." *Perspectives on Politics* 9(1): 25–43.

Index